# STORIES FROM THE SPIRITUAL LIFE

## – VOLUME I

### TEJVAN PETTINGER

Copyright © 2018 Tejvan Pettinger

No portion of this book may be reproduced in any form without express written permission from the publisher:

ISBN: 978-1-911319-21-4

# Table of contents

## Part I – In conversation

- Guru's boys — 10
- Bahir and Peter — 16
- The Master's physical presence — 18
- Joy — 24
- Difficulties in the spiritual life — 28
- Paper and scolding — 32
- Working for the Master — 40
- Coming to the spiritual life — 48
- Technology — 54
- Parents and the spiritual life — 58
- Imperfect disciples — 62
- Was life easier in the past? — 68
- Giving meditation classes — 74
- Helping at the race — 80
- Weekly meditations — 86
- Getting up early — 90

## Part II – Stories

- Lack of confidence — 100
- Choosing a path — 104
- Meditation and dedication — 108
- Working in the world — 112
- Misunderstanding — 116
- Living together — 118
- Singing with enthusiasm — 124
- Correcting others — 126
- Reincarnation — 130
- Inspired by sleeping disciples — 134
- Following the crowd — 136
- New disciples — 140
- God's love — 146

# Preface

These are a few stories inspired by following the spiritual life under the guidance of Sri Chinmoy. Some events are loosely based on real life; sometimes the stories just try to capture the spirit of the spiritual life according to my own understanding and perception.

There is a well-known story of five blind men coming across an elephant. Each man gives a different description of the elephant - one describes a tail, one describes a long bending trunk, another describes a thick, impenetrable hide. Each man is right from his particular perspective, but at the same time, none of them can see the totality of the elephant - let alone understand the inner beliefs and thinking of the elephant.

As disciples, we are sailing in the same boat; we can describe an aspect of our Master, which is correct from our limited perspective and personal filter, but this is just a glimpse into the life of the spiritual Master who is dealing with many layers of consciousness - mostly invisible to our outer eyes.

If the stories have any value and wisdom, I would like to give credit to my spiritual teacher, Sri Chinmoy. If the stories give any misleading impression or limited perspective, bear in mind, they are just a work in progress.

I did not set out to write a book. I just found that writing stories was a rewarding way to reflect on certain issues and experiences. The stories were also not written in chronological order. I started off by writing the stories in Part 2, but over time, found a lot of joy in writing conversations between different imaginary disciples. Perhaps sometimes a young Tejvan is speaking to an old Tejvan - you can make up your own mind!

Sometimes, I was surprised at how the conversations developed, and this reflects how it is in real life. If you start speaking about mundane things, your memory can be triggered and a story of the Master from many years ago comes to mind. This is the beauty of the spiritual life – it is all pervasive, and even in the most mundane activities, we can learn to see from a different perspective, which gives us much greater satisfaction and joy.

Tejvan Pettinger
Oxford, 24 May 2018

Spirituality is not like coasting
But exactly like climbing —
Climbing ten thousand Himalayas.

- Sri Chinmoy[1]

---

[1] Sri Chinmoy, *Ten Thousand Flower-Flames, part 58,* #5757
Agni Press, 1983.

# PART I

# IN CONVERSATION

# Guru's boys

A few years after his Master's passing Bahir asked his old friend Reynash, "What is your most memorable experiences from this lifetime?"

Reynash paused and went silent as if conjuring up some long treasured memory. After an effortless silence he spoke: "There was a time, in the very early days of the Ashram, when we were a small group of boys and we were living entirely for the Master. At every moment, we were thinking – what does the Master want us to do? But when I say thinking, that isn't the right word because we weren't sitting around mentally thinking – it was all intuition. We didn't need to think – we just did. Of course we were getting the Master's direct guidance, but sometimes all it needed was a glance, a smile, a frown and it was enough for us to know. We weren't going to the Master for every outer thing, but in spirit we were."

"We all got up early in the morning to meditate. The energy of those days made it hard to sleep in; the collective energy made it easy to get up. After meditation, we might run or play football or perhaps the Master wanted us to do something for him straight away. There was such a variety of work to do for the Master – building, fixing, publishing his writings. But work was an inadequate description. The Master was co-ordinating everything so it was something infinitely more fulfilling than a sense of work."

"The Master was always full of surprises. Sometimes he could be very strict; at other times, he would regale us with stories – stories from the early days or juicy anecdotes about his life or the world-situation. These little nuggets we loved. The Master's insights shone a light on the underlying forces shaping the world and stripped away the outer layers of deception and false motives. From these brief comments we glimpsed a small window into his inner life. To us, the Master's inner spiritual force and love felt more real and powerful than all the loud voices of the outer world combined. His real miracles we will never know."

"At the time, we had so much hope. I remember with great vividness the youthful energy of the boys – brimming with devotion and eagerness to please the Master – there was no thought of planning or pacing ourselves. There was also no sense of sacrifice or straining. We just felt grateful to be there – in that moment, at that particular place with our Master."

"If we had an evening free, we would bring musical instruments to the temple and we would sing bhajans late into the night. The so-called attractions of the world had no allure for us. It all felt grey and dreary compared to our life with the Master – it felt like we were in a giant bubble, protected and insulated from any outer temptations and pressures. We just went along with the flow, as if an invisible hand was carrying us along."

"In those days, we were always ready. If the Master asked, we just did. I remember one night being woken at 2.30am by Rajiv, saying we had to go right away to the Master's compound to start building a temporary kitchen for some visitors who were coming later in the day. I don't know why we had to start at that time, but we just saw it as an adventure and threw ourselves into the task. It was in these unplanned moments that you felt something different – something special that could not be achieved through comfortable routines. Working late into the night to finish something brought a great sense of teamwork and self-transcendence. We gave little thought to our own comfort."

"I remember once the Master organised a race – 2 miles I think it was. And when we got to the start line, the Master said with a smile, 'Is it only 2 miles? My favourite number is seven, let us make it a 7-mile race!' And when we finished – exhausted and spent – the Master said to us, 'Could you not run another three miles and make it double digits – 10 miles?' The Master was always gently pushing us out of our comfort zone. Nothing of Ashram life was fixed or set in stone – the Master never allowed us to be caught by the mind's rigidity."

Arnav jumped into the conversation, "Yes. I remember once we were sitting with the Master on a hot day, and the Master suddenly jumped up and said, 'I'm going for a walk, you can follow 10 metres behind.' So we set off without thought for provisions or any preparation. We literally followed in the Master's footsteps. Now, after we had been walking for an hour or two, the Ashram is out of sight and we are deep into the hilly terrain that surrounds the Ashram, and for the first time, my faith starts to waiver – and I'm thinking to myself, 'I'm thirsty, hungry, and I haven't even got my proper walking shoes on.' But, the Master is in full flight, and we are having to really strive to keep up with his relentless pace.

Then, as the sun reaches its peak, we stumble across a small isolated cottage and the Master momentarily pauses. Out of the cottage come an elderly couple who look excited – as if they are ready to meet us – and they welcome the Master and say, 'This morning we felt a strong desire to feed spiritual pilgrims.' And so with mutual joy they invite us into their small cottage and garden and we can quench our thirst. In that scorching heat – with our Master in a joyful mood – the refreshments have never tasted so sweet. And so we continue our journey into the dense undergrowth of the bush – up and down ravines, always following the Master who is blazing a trail in front of us. After the morning's serendipity, we dismiss our fears and worries and just walk on – living every moment of this great adventure. After many twists and turns, and seemingly forever lost in the wild landscape of the surrounding hills, we descend a hill, to see the Ashram shining in the evening sun. What a welcome sight! We return to the Ashram with a deep sense of satisfaction."

"The Master is happy, and for the rest of the evening he invites spiritual questions and we talk late into the night. As the day of unimaginable rich events draws to a close, we are tired, aching, but inwardly full. And, just as we turn to retire for the night, the Master gives a parting shot, 'In the spiritual life, always we have to be ready to drop everything and follow the Master. You might not be able to see where I am going, but believe me I have travelled these paths many times and I do know how to take you to the destination – the destination of our Beloved Lord Supreme.' But then, without taking a breath, the Master says: 'Tomorrow morning I would like us to have a 5-mile race at 6 in the morning. So go get some rest!' That's how the Master was and, of course, still is. Never rest on your laurels. Always it is about the present moment, the next achievement."

There was a pause and then Reynash picked up his flow again, "I don't remember any jealousy or jostling for position – those things seemed unimportant, irrelevant. In those days we all felt a closeness to the Master – whether he spoke to us or not. We also had a fearlessness, which came from our living faith in the Master. Once the Master was expecting a visitor from overseas. He really wanted us to fix the potholes in the local public road. So we went down to the local council, beseeching and imploring. But even our faith and lobbying couldn't move the bureaucratic wheels of local government. When we told the Master, he looked non-plussed and he just turned around and asked, 'Could you not fix them yourself?'"

"Of course, we have no idea how to fix potholes or whether it is legal to do so. So we just go out and buy some tar and cones and start fixing the potholes in the road, with disciples directing the traffic, whilst we close off half the road. We work hard for two solid days and no one seems to say anything. But, as we nearly finish, a very official looking person comes storming up to us – asking what on earth we were doing! We could have been in trouble, but the Master's grace is there and this furious official is quietly charmed by our innocence and lack of guile. He can't believe. So this is what happens – rather than getting arrested, he says he will make a call and try ask his council men to come with a steam roller and finish off the job."

"That was the spirit which we had – we had a simple childlike faith. Everything was for the Master."

"So what happened next?" asked Bahir.

"Well, we got older for a start!" said Reynash.

"Sorry, I didn't mean it like that," said Bahir.

"I know. But, also, it is true; that intensity did almost imperceptibly fade. It faded so gradually, you didn't notice. But, when I look back, quite a few of those divine qualities gradually diminished. Perhaps human nature can only progress so far in one incarnation. That is human life. Don't get me wrong, the spiritual life has still been very fruitful, but I suppose you can't always progress at the fastest speed."

"Many years later, rather ruefully, the Master said, 'If you can't be happy in my own way, at least be happy in your own way.' The Master's love and concern was of course still there, but we were now travelling in the slower lane – not the express lane that the Master really hoped we would."

"But, those days remain etched in my memory – which in itself is a blessing, because it can become easy to forget or even doubt our own spiritual experiences. The Master said any spiritual experience will always be part of our soul, and in the future, when we come back, these spiritual achievements will be there waiting to be rediscovered. As you get close to the end of life, you will realise these spiritual experiences are the only thing you can really take with you."

"Bahir, when you feel the inner fire, don't wait for anyone. Don't look back. Just go forward."

# Bahir and Peter

Many years later, Bahir was now 78 years old and had been following the spiritual life for nearly 60 years. Although his body was increasingly frail, the short time he spent with his Master all those years ago was still a very vivid and living reality.

Peter, a young disciple of the Master, was keen to hear stories from one of the very few remaining disciples to have seen the Master in the physical.

"Peter, it's so kind of you to come and visit an old man like me," said Bahir.

"Not at all," said Peter. "You know how much I love to hear stories from a disciple who was there with the Master. Even the smallest nugget or recollection about our Master can be very meaningful."

"Yes, it's true," said Bahir. "Even after all these years, I can remember a single glance or word from my Master with such an intense reality. When our Master was in the physical so many things we took for granted; he brought down so much light – we often struggled to assimilate and appreciate all that he was doing. Even 30 or 40 years after his passing, I started to understand for the first time a teaching he gave so many years ago."

"But, don't overly value the experiences of an ageing man; I often feel the disciples who came after the Master's physical passing have more love and more devotion than we ever did, and that devotion is much more important than juicy stories from the past."

"Bahir, today I have come with a tape recorder to capture as many stories as you are able to share," said Peter.

"Well Peter, I can try. Remember I didn't actually spend much time with the Master. As you know, many of my stories are second-hand and filtered through my own perspective. So you can take them with a pinch of salt. Also, as you know, sometimes I can't help sharing stories that are nothing more than the product of my over-active imagination. If they have any truth or relevance to our path – your heart can decide!"

"Yes, I appreciate that, but at the same time, I get so much joy to hear these stories," said Peter.

Bahir smiled. "You many not believe it Peter, but you remind me very much of myself 50 years ago. Then, how many hours I spent talking with older disciples – encouraging them to share any stories about the Master."

"Once our Master said that some of his disciples would live a very long time and our soul would not leave the body until we accomplished everything we had promised to do. I think this is why the Supreme is keeping me on earth for such a long time! I did do a few things, true, but I could have done a lot more."

"Perhaps relating these stories is the last thing I have to do. So Peter, make sure you remember to press the record button!"

# The Master's physical presence

Peter asked Bahir, "What was it like meeting the Master in person?"

"It's hard to know where to start," said Bahir. "The first thing is that it depended on your own state of consciousness. My own experience was that if you were receptive and inwardly quiet, then being with the Master could help you to have a good meditation and feel uplifted. When you were in the Master's presence, it could feel like you were walking into a spiritually charged atmosphere. Some days you felt it more than others, but seeing the Master in the physical always gave a sense of confidence that the spiritual life was something very real and ultimately something we could achieve too."

"It could feel so powerful near the Master's presence, there used to be a little competition to get the best seats in the room. I suppose seated nearer the front you had a better view and you could perhaps feel the Master's inner presence even more strongly. Of course, when I say 'competition to get the best seats', everyone was in their highest spirit of detachment and surrender." Bahir said with a smile.

"I know what you mean," said Peter with a smile, "Just like when I go around asking for volunteers to set up the kitchen in the early morning – it's almost like I don't need to ask,"

"Peter, you have a thankless task, but for this kind of service, I'm sure you will have a good seat in Heaven."

"Well, I don't know about that," said Peter, "but I suppose it is an opportunity for progress."

"Yes," said Bahir. "The Master once said that he will never remain indebted to us – either on the inner plane or the outer plane. Whatever service we offer, the Master will appreciate. The important thing is that nothing goes unrecorded. Every action, every thought, every motive is witnessed by God, and even the smallest action can have a ripple effect on other people, our future, the world – far beyond our imagination. It is not necessarily big actions, but even small words of kindness – or inwardly offering good will and harmony to our fellow disciples can have unimaginable importance to our Master's mission."

"The Master once said if you want to be a first-class disciple, 'never do anything you wouldn't be willing to do in front of him.' That is what we have to try and aspire for. Outwardly, we may gain no recognition or appreciation, but we have to feel that the Master is inwardly there – observing and encouraging every divine thought, word and action. Outer appearances don't always tell the full story. We may feel that our outer task is not glamorous or not fully appreciated, but in the inner world, we can have no idea who is really close to the Master and who is making a sterling contribution to the Master's Mission."

"Yes, said Peter. "When I'm in a good frame of mind, I don't worry about reward or recognition; I feel that the service is its own reward. Though, at the same time, it is nice to be appreciated occasionally."

"Going back to your question," said Bahir. "If you had an opportunity to sit at the Master's feet, it was an unimaginable opportunity. I remember once the Master invited disciples to come and sit on the floor – in front of the Master. Now, I had a nice comfortable seat, and I didn't feel inspired to move. I preferred to sit in my comfy chair because I thought a comfy chair equals better meditation – but some disciples literally started running down as soon as the Master finished speaking. Later on that day, the Master said that those disciples who came to sit on the floor were doing the right thing. The Master said you could get much more by being at the Master's feet – even if it is a little physically uncomfortable. Needless to say, I felt a little embarrassed sitting in my comfy chair!"

"Thank you for sharing that story," said Peter. "Although we can no longer literally sit at the Master's feet, I still feel that teaching is very applicable today. Sometimes to sit at the Master's feet – to follow the spiritual life according to the Master's own way – we sometimes have to endure a little outer discomfort."

"Yes, Peter. You are right. Everything the Master did in the physical has an equal relevance to our spiritual life at this very moment. The Master is definitely here in spirit. And as you suggest, the Master said the spiritual life is definitely not just about choosing the most comfortable and easy approach. Though, of course, we don't go to the other extreme of inviting suffering. Always we have to cultivate cheerfulness and joy, but sometimes we need to follow what our heart tells us is right – even if outwardly it is quite a challenging path."

"To see the Master in meditation or to hear him speak was a tremendous inspiration – we were so fortunate to have this opportunity, but also it is worth bearing in mind that being in the Master's presence was no panacea. If you went into the meditation room with jealousy, insecurity, and if you were unable to give these emotions up, then it was very difficult to feel the usual presence of the Master, and your meditation could be futile. If there was a little receptivity, the Master could lift us up, but only if we had that openness and receptivity."

"The Buddha once told a story that when he gave a lecture, quite a few different people came to listen – a thief, a sincere seeker, a gambler and so on. Now after the Buddha's lecture, what did they do? The thief went back to stealing, the gambler went gambling, and the sincere seeker went to pray and meditate. In other words, just listening to a spiritual Master's talk is not enough – we need the willingness to actually make the Master's teaching part of our life, and actually work on changing our nature. The spiritual Master can inspire those who are sincere, but we have to meet the Master part of the way. Our Master called it receptivity, and we all went through different periods of receptivity and openness. But, if you could go to the Master without expectation and without demands, then you definitely felt your own meditation could be lifted up."

"Also, sometimes I went to the Master's Ashram with many problems going around in my mind, and I felt a little hesitant, thinking: how am I going to get into a good meditation, with all these mental challenges? But, when you get to the Ashram and you meet your good friends, you get absorbed in the atmosphere of the place, and then a lot of your problems start to slip away."

"I know what you mean," said Peter; "sometimes I'm reluctant to travel because it seems a lot of effort, and I get caught up in my daily work. But, when I do make it, I'm always relieved that I actually made it. I think when you get caught up in your daily life, it is very easy to forget how beautiful it is to enter into that spiritual vibration," "Yes. I think the difficulty is that visiting the Master's main ashram is very much an experience of the heart and soul. When our mind thinks about it, it is hard for the mind to understand that the shift in consciousness makes everything so different. Quite often I think I have serious problems, but when I spend time in the Master's Ashram, I look back and think: why did I worry about these problems? The issues are still the same, but you're in a different consciousness. And it is this consciousness that helps solve our problems."

Bahir continued, "I remember the last time I saw my Master in the physical. It was a very soulful moment. We just walked past in silent meditation. The Master seemed lost – deep in trance. It looked like the Master was only keeping a small part of his consciousness on earth. I felt he was immersed in the spiritual world Beyond, and yet the Master was still here as a bridge between Heaven and earth – giving a glimpse into that world, which is beyond thought and the cares of human life. At the time, I never imagined it would be the last time I saw the Master in the physical. But it has remained etched in my memory. I try tell myself whatever we go through here on earth, it is only a temporary experience."

Peter asked, "Is it different visiting the Master's Ashram now the Master is no longer in the physical?"

"Yes and no," said Bahir. "When the Master left the body, I realised good meditations were not dependent on how close you were to the Master's physical body. I'm not trying to boast, but in all honesty, I have had deeper and more fruitful meditations since the Master's physical passing. Inwardly I feel the Master's consciousness as strongly as before – if not more so. But, of course, some things are different. The Master in the physical was the most beautiful thing – it was so easy to be inspired and give more importance to our spiritual life. The Master was always willing to encourage, scold and inspire us to take the spiritual life more seriously, more soulfully – and whatever the Master said, it was always accompanied with that intangible spiritual energy that helped you to make real changes in your life. Now the Master is no longer in the physical, you have to work just a little harder to motivate yourself and maintain that spiritual discipline. But, at the same time, if we do work harder, we make our spiritual muscles stronger. When the Master was in the physical, in a way you could say we were spoilt. Like the Master giving prasad by hand, the Master giving us individual meditations. With all these spiritual riches, it could feel like all you had to do was turn up. Now we have to be more conscious and try to remember the Master is literally right here with us, behind that thinner than the thinnest veil between Heaven and earth."

"I know what you mean," said Peter, "sometimes on special celebration days of the Master, this thin veil itself seems to dissolve – giving you at least one foot into Heaven."

"Yes, we are so fortunate," said Bahir. "I feel the Master's Ashram is a place of living divinity on earth. No matter what we go through, just visiting the meditation park and Ashram gardens can save us. It has been a constant oasis in this world of change and suffering."

# Joy

"How was your last weekend trip?" asked Peter.

Bahir replied, "Well, travelling isn't easy but it was great to make the weekend retreat. The disciples had organised meditations, singing, games and more. That was all fine, but after the final meditation, the main organiser announced, 'Now we are very lucky to have Bahir today. Bahir has been following the spiritual life for 60 years [cheers from the audience!] and he spent considerable time with the Master in the physical. Now Bahir is kindly going to come up and share a few stories.'"

"Well, that was a fine thing! I felt a knot in my stomach; nobody had told me this was on the programme. Speaking to groups of five or six people is one thing. But, 600+ people – well there should be a law against it at my age! But, before I had time to think and run for cover, my old friend Malin put a microphone in my face."

"Now, here's a tip for you Peter. If you're not sure what to say, try a bit of flattery! Always goes down well. So I start by appreciating the energy and enthusiasm of the disciples – of course flattery is much easier if it is genuinely true! Anyway, I flounder around and say the first things that come to my mind.

"I'm sure it wasn't that bad," said Peter.

"Yes. I think it went down OK. What I said was something like this: "I have truly enjoyed this weekend of spiritual activities. It is also a great encouragement to see a new generation of disciples coming to the fore who are a shining example of how our Master is very much with us in spirit."

"As you know, I'm a very old man, but the thing I enjoyed absolutely the most at this weekend were the fun games. At least the ones that didn't involve running! The Master would often say when the disciples had this kind of innocent joy, it was a great weight off his shoulders."

"It reminds me of a story many years ago. We were with our Master in a foreign country and after a soulful morning meditation, there was free time in the afternoon. One group of boys began to play football and had an epic two-hour game. Nearby, another group of boys had a meeting on the grass where they talked about future projects to spread the Master's light. Now it happened that those in the meeting were disturbed by the football game and so one of those disciples complained to the Master that their meeting had been disrupted."

"However, the Master didn't react as they expected. The Master said, 'The boys playing football are doing absolutely the right thing. By playing football, so many wrong forces and negative thoughts they are leaving behind on the pitch. I appreciate the intent of those disciples trying to spread my light. But, everything has its time and place. It's a beautiful afternoon; we should take the opportunity for sport and relaxation. Also, forgive me for saying, but when I hear the word 'meeting', in no way does it inspire me! Did the great Swami Vivekananda shake up the world by having meetings and talking about his plans? No. Vivekananda simply did. So please don't worry about planning and discussing – instead just throw yourself into self-giving service.'"

"It reminds me of another time when I was seeing the Master for the first or second time. Disciples from our country were honouring, in a light-hearted fashion, some achievement of the Master whilst he was visiting New Zealand. I can't remember why, but someone had the idea to put white socks on our ears so we would look like sheep while performing."

"In all sincerity, I thought this was absolutely the worst idea. I was seeing my Master for the first time, and here I was putting socks on my ears. One or two of the older disciples refused, and I would have joined them, but I was a new disciple so I went along with it. Well, after the performance, the Master smiled, and he gently teased those older disciples who were standing at the end of the line: 'Eh Taruk and Gopal, do you not have any ears, like everyone else!?' Now whether the Master genuinely appreciated our costume or not, we will never know. He wouldn't always say what he really felt about performances! But I felt I did the right thing by joining in with the spirit of the performance – even if my mind didn't fully agree!"

"On that first trip to meet my Master, I learnt that everything has its time and place. A few days later we were performing some soulful songs at an evening meditation. We dressed in immaculate white clothes and, before going on stage, we meditated in silence for a minute. The short five-minute performance was a most soulful and memorable experience. The Master was in a sublime trance, and I was deeply moved by the atmosphere and ineffable peace emanating from the Master's presence. After the performance concluded, there was an indescribable hush as we absorbed the Master's final moments of silence. I felt I had climbed up at least half a step to Heaven and, as I went back to my seat, I sat in silence trying to absorb the experience."

"My good friend Jahangir once told me an illumining story. He was with the Master and a few disciples seated on the curb of a pavement. The Master suddenly said, 'Please try go into your highest meditation.' So the boys tried to meditate to their best of their ability. Then after a few minutes, the Master said, 'Jahangir, please tell us a funny joke,' which he did, and then the Master said, 'Now please try go back to your highest meditation.' Then after a few minutes, he asked for a joke. Like this, it went on – high meditation, then humour."

"What was the Master trying to achieve with this unique experience? The way I understand it, the Master wanted to show us that we shouldn't limit the spiritual life and try putting into a neat box. Spirituality is not just sitting at our shrine and meditating for a set number of minutes. We always have to be ready to do what our Master wants. If the Master wants us to meditate, we should put our heart and soul into meditation. If the Master wants us to put on plays or tell jokes, we should put our heart and soul into that. Above all, the Master's path is not about following our own preconceptions of what we think spirituality should be. The final thing is that everything has its time and place. Serious and soulful meditation is an absolute necessity in the spiritual life, but humour and innocent fun also have their role. If we are always serious, we can become dry and inflexible. If we are always joking, there is no soulfulness or devotion. We shouldn't neglect either. The spiritual life needs balance."

"If there is one thing I miss about the Master leaving the body, it is that spontaneity and the variety of divine moods the Master could display. Some days the Master would come to our meeting place and it would be real seriousness – soulful meditation, lofty, illumining talks – and you felt the presence of divine light, divine transformation and your own eager promise to make a renewed commitment to the spiritual life. But, on other days, the Master would come and it would be all sweetness – 'juicy stories', humorous skits and innocent fun. Then the Master became like a grandfather figure – all compassion, love and forgiveness."

"Sometimes we would get these different aspects all within the same day. You never knew what was coming next – it was impossible to predict. You just entered into the flow of the Master's energy."

# Difficulties in the spiritual life

"Bahir, I admire your poise and cheerfulness. It seems the spiritual life comes so effortlessly to you," said Peter.

"Peter, you are very perceptive," said Bahir. "My Master always said I was a very good actor!"

"Well, I suppose after 60 years on the spiritual path, you hope to make at least a little progress! But when I was a fairly new disciple – even when I was on the path for many years – quite a few difficult periods I had. In all honesty, I never lost faith in God or my Master's divinity, but sometimes I felt a disconnect between the spiritual life and my state of mind. Everywhere I saw problems, difficulties and a heavy weight in my mind, but at the same time, it seemed everyone else seemed to be so effortlessly spiritual and cheerful!"

"When I felt this inner frustration, my instinct was to retreat into a shell – be quiet, stop going to things, try to lose myself in television, etc. Now looking back, I feel that it is exactly those times when you want to retreat into a shell that it becomes more important than ever to keep going to activities in the Ashram."

"When we mull over our problems, we just make them stronger. It is like trying to clean your room with a dirty broom. It just spreads the dirt around. The best thing is to go out and buy a new broom."

"One occasion I remember. I had planned to go to one of our Ashram's weekend retreats. But because I felt so lousy, I cancelled. I couldn't face it. I received one or two messages encouraging me to go, but I just ignored. Subconsciously I was probably proud of my decision to stay home and sulk. But on Friday evening, old Gopal came round and he just started talking about the weather, football – silly stuff. And then, despite my deepest resistance, I caught some of his infectious cheerfulness, and it was just enough to shift my frame of mind."

"Then – as if he perceived the subtle shift in my mind – he said with a big inviting grin, 'Now, dear Bahir, are you not coming with us this weekend? It will all be great fun.' His sympathetic oneness and abiding good-nature broke through my pride, and it seemed foolish to stay home and be miserable. So I changed my mind."

"But the next day, I get on the train and the old demons return. It is the disconnect between reality and where you think you should be. It can be a little bit intimidating going to social occasions when you're feeling low. But, I remembered a teaching of my Master: 'If you are depressed, just pretend to be happy. If you don't feel happy, force yourself to give a fake smile.' The Master said that from this fake happiness, you can start to believe your own acting; and, when you're with your friends, their cheerfulness and good nature will lift you up. So even if we feel down, we just need to turn up and try to cultivate a little cheerfulness – even if it is not a particularly sincere happiness, the Master will take care of the rest."

"Peter, when you're 80 years old, you will never look back and say to yourself: 'If only I stayed at home a bit more often!' Now my only regret is not doing more. When I was a young disciple, we had so many opportunities to see the Master in person, and what did I do? I thought about my bank balance and whether I could afford. Now my bank account has accumulated very nicely, but when you're hobbling around like me, what use are savings? Money can't bring back these unbelievable missed opportunities.

"Do you really regret so much?" Peter asked.

"No. As the Master says, 'Regret is worse than useless.' But, as a great spiritual Master once said: it is a good philosophy not to worry about the tomorrow. In the spiritual life, live in the moment. When you have the enthusiasm and aspiration, just live the spiritual life to its full. Don't think: if you can only accumulate more money, you will be able to retire early and devote your life to meditation. It doesn't work like that. I doubt God gives better meditations just because you have saved more for your retirement fund!"

Peter asked: "What would the Master say about overcoming depression and unhappiness?"

"Well, this conversation reminds me of the times when I was with the Master. When we had walking meditation – which involved walking past the Master – on quite a few occasions the Master would say, 'Please smile when you go past. Please offer your most soulful smile. And if you can't offer a soulful smile, at least try to offer a fake smile.' Again the Master said: if we start off with a fake smile and an iota of receptivity, then we can start to receive a little of the Master's light. But, if we are depressed, the Master's light cannot penetrate and we will get nothing. The Master always said the spiritual life is not about austerity and long faces. Cheerfulness is supremely important in our spiritual life and it is something we should always try to cultivate. But, of course, so many challenges we get in life; the spiritual life is no different. A useful analogy is to think of water. If it stays still, the water becomes stagnant; by contrast the flowing water of a stream brings freshness and clarity. When we are depressed, that is the time to really make an effort to do something positive. At this time, don't worry about trying to have your best meditation. Go for a run, get involved in selfless service, spend time with your friends; these physical actions have the capacity to lift us out of our ego's shell. When we get our life-energy back, then you will find you start to get your meditation back too."

"Now, Peter, this is a bit of philosophy I have made up. So you can treat it with the respect it deserves."

"90% of the spiritual life is turning up," Bahir laughed to himself.

"Now you might say this is foolish, but I feel if I turn up at my shrine daily, if I turn up for selfless services, if I turn up for weekly meditation, then at least I'm in the right boat and it is the job of the boatman to take me to the other shore."

"Of course, I'm not saying you can go to meditation and then have a nice sleep because you have done your job of turning up! We have to aspire too."

"Yes Bahir, I know what you mean. It makes sense." said Peter.

"Very good Peter, but I hope by now you have learnt not to take anything I say too seriously!"

# Paper and scolding

A piece of paper was blown off the table and Bahir bent down to pick it up. But, before his aching joints could lift him from the chair, Peter had leapt down to pick it up.

Peter asked. "I notice you are always quick to pick up any paper from the floor. Is there a reason?"

"Yes," said Bahir. "Well, firstly it wasn't always like that – you should have seen my student flat! But our Master taught us that paper has a sacred quality. The source of paper and books is the goddess of learning – Saraswati – so we have to treat with great respect. Also, if we appreciate and value paper, then it also helps to us to be more receptive to the inner wisdom and knowledge. Once my friend Malin, who worked selling the Master's books, was carrying some cardboard boxes when they started falling over – so he kicked them to get them back on the trolley. The Master happened to see and he called out, 'Malin! What are you doing? You should never kick those boxes - unless you want to be born without any intelligence in your next incarnation.' As it happened the boxes were empty, but it was a reminder the Master cared about every detail of life – but especially how we treat his books and writings."

"In the hoary past, spiritual Masters didn't write – they only spread their teachings by their inner silence and the spoken word. But, there came a time when the spoken word and aural teachings were no longer enough. So sacred texts were created. Our Master said God gave paper a sacred quality to capture and transfer the light of the spiritual Masters. The teachings of spiritual Masters are not just about the words they use, but the light and consciousness they inject into them. An ordinary person could write a similar philosophy, but the consciousness is different to when a realised soul writes."

"Of course these days you can read everything on an electronic screen, but the screen doesn't capture this inner light in the same way. That is why I read the Master's work in paper form."

Peter said, "Just looking at your library and all those original books gives me such great joy."

"Yes, the Master says a physical book carries the consciousness of the writer. As you know, the Master encouraged us to read every day, but once he said: if you really can't read, at least look at my books! Can you believe? I was so happy to hear that because sometimes I'm too tired to read, but I have spent many hours rearranging these books and just looking at them."

"Once I made a vow to read not only all the Master's books, but also all the pamphlets, programmes, notes – everything. Once I was reading a small pamphlet that listed some notes the Master had made about his travels. The content was very plain and to be honest a bit repetitive. At the start of reading the pamphlet, I thought: why am I reading this? It is not his lofty poems or lectures; just relatively mundane notes. But, I persevered and tried to keep a quiet mind. And then, I had the feeling of being transported to one of the Master's lectures. It was like I was there at the back of the room – absorbing the spiritual intensity and the air of eager anticipation I remember so many years ago. You might say the experience was mental hallucination, but I did feel something."

"Which reminds me. Once an old disciple, who has since passed up to Heaven, told me that the Master said we should preserve everything – everything in its exact original form – because you have no idea what seemingly small thing will enable future seekers and disciples to access the Master's consciousness."

"It reminds me of the time I once visited a good friend Amar. In his room was a framed letter, which was typed by Amar, and a few handwritten comments in reply by the Master. Amar had asked his Master about a most significant project. Due to outer difficulties, Amar wasn't sure whether to go ahead or not. He explained the situation and offered the Master three options. Next to the option of doing nothing and delaying until next year, the Master had written in a bold, confident script just one word – 'Absurd!!!'

"When I saw this original handwriting of the Master, such a powerful experience I felt! It was like the Master was standing right beside you, giving you a ten-minute talk. From this one word it seemed to convey everything you needed to know. It captured the consciousness of the Master: Go forward! Don't delay! Don't make excuses! From this piece of paper, so much inspiration I got, and it remains vivid in my memory. Now on its own, what does that word mean? Nothing. But, in that context – seeing the Master's handwriting on paper – it transferred so much."

"It is not just paper that we should respect. The Master said that everything has a soul. If we treat physical objects as inanimate, lifeless things, this is a limited understanding. If you leave clothes, crumpled, dirty on the floor, and walk over them, will they like it? But, if you look after and treasure objects, you will start to feel a subtle difference. If we are callous towards our physical objects, which help us through life, this callousness can permeate into other aspects of our life too. Even with objects in our house, we can exercise the capacity of our heart."

"When I joined the spiritual path, this perspective I definitely didn't have. But I picked things up from other disciples and I read a book by a Japanese monk about how treasuring objects could be an integral part of a spiritual life. When I tried to change my attitude, I realised you could have such a different way of looking at the world. Slowly, I felt more meaning in even everyday chores. If we treasure things, they last longer. Also, if we treat objects badly, they are more likely to break, get lost or worse. And this reminds me of a story, which is both embarrassing and perhaps for you funny."

"One weekend I was inwardly cursing the ubiquitous role of smartphones in the modern world. Go to the gym, church, café - and it seems everyone has their head glued to a screen. And if you have a meditation with 500 people, you will always be blessed with at least one irritating noise emanating from these machines. As you know Peter, I'm a grumpy old man so I can say these things!"

"Anyway, I'm a very bad, hopeless disciple and I allow these things to get me frustrated. Now Peter, you might be thinking – what's wrong with me? I don't know! But, at that particular time, I was ruminating a lot on this issue. Anyway, that weekend, for some reason, I'm inspired to sit in the front row during our meditation. I don't know why. Usually, I sit at the back. On the front row, you can feel more exposed – as if the Master's inner presence is examining your alertness even more intensely. You don't want to fall asleep on the front row!"

"Without fail, I always switch my phone to airplane mode. Usually, I like to switch off for the whole weekend – it's a relief to be free of notifications, at least for one day a week."

"So, here I am in the front row, enjoying a deeply soulful performance from the top female singers in the Ashram. I'm in a deep meditation, my whole centre of being is in the heart – the mind is barely functioning and I feel this powerful joy in the heart."

"Alas, the curse of the modern age strikes again! Not a ringtone, but like a morning alarm – some harsh, discordant bell. Its irritating tones disturb the profound sense of peace and I feel the re-awakening of the mind. I try to surreptitiously look around to eye the offending person and offer them my inner blessings – while at the same time pretending to still meditate."

"There is no movement – as if everyone is trying to pretend it's not happening. Like the proverbial pink elephant in the room, it's so discordant you want to disbelieve your own senses."

"Now at the third ring, the sudden painful realisation – the offending phone is in my pocket! My heart sinks through to the floor, and I try to simultaneously turn it off as quickly as possible, while also making a pathetic attempt to pretend I'm not actually moving. Exposed, I half expect the singers to stop mid-performance while 500 pairs of disapproving eyes turn on me until I have completed the manoeuvre. But, fortunately, everyone else is keeping the same pretence of still being deep in trance!"

"Whether these machines have a soul, God alone knows – but on that morning they had their revenge! Now, even 50 years later, I still try to defend myself. Never in the past year had I set any kind of alarm – I bought a clock specifically so I wouldn't be dependent on a smart-computer for every aspect of life from dawn to dusk. What quirk of fate that this machine was able to set itself to go off on this date, this time and this place!"

"I would like to say I never cursed the smartphone again, but unfortunately that lesson I didn't learn!"

"What would the Master do if a phone went off like that?" asked Peter.

"That is a very good question," said Bahir, "and I really don't know the answer. The Master may ignore it, he could make light of, scold the individual or scold all the disciples and remind them they shouldn't be bringing in these machines to the meditation room. It would depend very much on timing, circumstance and the people involved."

"I suppose now it is all philosophical speculation, but seated in the front row, I felt or imagined the Master's inner scolding."

"Even 50 years after the Master's mahasamadhi, I miss the Master's physical presence with such intensity it is hard to explain. But, on that particular day, I suppose I was relieved the Master wasn't sitting two metres away. I might have died of embarrassment."

"But, even though we don't have the Master's outer blessing-scoldings, I feel it is very good to be asking the question as you did – how would the Master respond? It's not a question of worrying about getting the right answer. But, it means we are trying to feel the Master's inner presence, observing our every action."

"In that particular case, I could justify myself by saying it was really bad luck. It was not intentional carelessness. But, also you might ask: why did I get bad luck?"

"If my Master had scolded me for carelessness and disturbing the peace of the meditation, definitely I would have taken it to heart and felt it was something I deserved."

"In that particular case, it is true I was not intentionally careless – you might sympathise and say it was bad luck. But, other times I know carelessness creeps into my life and I get away with it because my brother disciples cover for me."

"It reminds me of a story. Once a disciple close to the Master – Ventri – was scolded by the Master for some carelessness in the Ashram. Now Ventri took the scolding with folded hands and a devotional attitude. He did not say anything."

"Now, it happened that a few days later the Master found out that Ventri was actually in no way responsible. So he spoke to Ventri and asked: 'So Ventri, when I scolded you and it was not your fault, why did you not say anything?' and Ventri replied, 'Well, although I was not responsible on this occasion, I probably deserved it for other occasions of carelessness, which did not come to light.' The Master was very happy and spoke to all the disciples, 'Here Ventri is doing absolutely the right thing. Because he took my scolding in the right spirit, he became receptive to my transformation-light and will make real progress. Sometimes when I scold disciples it is all excuses and self-justification. But this is the wrong attitude – if you try to deflect the Master's scolding you are blocking my love, concern and light. When I scold you people, believe me, I suffer much more than you do. These scoldings are the proof that I really love you and care for your nature's transformation. My only real punishment is my indifference. So always be open and see scoldings as a vehicle for the transformation of your ego.'

"That is so beautiful," mentioned Peter.

"Yes, the Master is no longer in the physical, but this inner attitude of self-awareness we have to maintain. It does not mean we become overly critical. We have to love ourselves in a divine way. If we really love the real in us, we will try to transform our nature."

"And, Peter, always make sure you turn your phone off!"

# Working for the Master

There was a knock at the door and another old man entered the room. Although he was hobbling very slowly, his face was beaming with happiness.

Bahir said: "Hey Chetan, it's great to see you!"

"Now Peter, here is the proof – another disciple older than me. Can you believe?"

"Chetan, Peter here has been skilfully getting me to tell stories from the days with our Master."

Chetan sat down and said, "Very nice to meet you, Peter. Bahir is a good chap, but when it comes to telling stories – well he has a much better memory than me! And if I may say, he does add his own rhetorical flourishes every now and then – things no one else seems to remember!"

Bahir replied: "But, Chetan, you spent much more time with the Master in the physical, I'm sure you have a few good stories to share."

Peter asked eagerly: "Perhaps you could say how you came to the Master's path."

Chetan laughed and said, "Well, I suppose I got lucky! My parents joined the Ashram when I was a young boy. So my skill or luck – whatever you want to call it – was being born into a spiritual family."

Peter admired the energy and warmth of this old man and asked, "So how was it growing up on the Master's path!?"

"For me, the Master's path is all about joy," said Chetan. "When we were growing up we had so much fun with different activities. The Master was very skilled at keeping us busy. In this vortex of energy and activity, the spiritual life felt so natural – it didn't feel like a life of discipline; we were just always looking forward to the time when we could visit the Ashram or travel with the Master."

"Now Bahir, I bet he's been telling you all about the Master's strictness, but to me, the Master was so affectionate, loving and to us quite tolerant – especially when we were growing up. It was amazing when you think how the Master was so accepting of so many different characters within the Ashram. With our mind, we judge people, but the Master saw the soul's potential and always encouraged us with love and affection."

"Well I do remember some times when the Master wasn't always so tolerant with us," interjected Bahir.

Chetan threw back his head and laughed heartily. "Good old Bahir. You can always rely on him to remember the Master's scoldings!" I'm sure in a previous incarnation he was a monk."

Bahir smiled and added: "Well, I don't know about that. I always thought in my previous incarnation I might have been an entertainer or comedian. But for this incarnation the Supreme – out of His infinite Compassion – took away my charisma and comedic capacity. Otherwise, I may never have made it to the spiritual life, but ended up as a famous entertainer again!"

"Well Bahir, the Supreme certainly did a good job in taking away your comic timing. If anyone can make a great joke fall flat, it is your good self. I still think you were a monk."

With a smile, Bahir replied, "Well, Chetan my dear friend, you have inspired me to tell a joke."

"O dear, here we go!" said Chetan, as he put his head in his hands.

Bahir ignored his friend's low expectations and turned to Peter – who seemed a more willing listener.

"Did you hear about the dentist who took up meditation? [dramatic pause] He became an expert in Transcendental medication."

Bahir looked pleased with himself, Peter politely laughed and Chetan groaned. "O dear, Bahir, I think that joke is older than your own good self. I'm not even sure if you got the ending right."

Peter feared more one-liners might be coming so he took the opportunity to ask the newcomer, "Chetan, may I ask what it was like working on projects with the Master?"

"Yes," said Chetan. "When the Master started a project, he was all enthusiasm and eagerness, and above all he wanted it done sooner than the soonest. When he gave instructions, the Master would ask, 'How long will it take?' And we might reply, 'Five days, Guru.' And the Master would reply, 'Can you not do it in three?' We would think it impossible, but we knew by experience, the Master always had other ideas and so we would reply. 'We will try, Guru.' Then after the first day, the Master would be ringing and asking, 'Is it finished yet?' It was an exhilarating experience working for the Master.

"When we worked, our good friend Virat would be in charge of the project. He could be a hard taskmaster – because he felt all the responsibility. Once a project started there was little time for meditation and relaxation. Our work became our meditation. When I think back and consider the hours we worked, my mind is amazed. But, at the time, you didn't think – you just got into the Master's flow and time just sped by. Whenever we seemed to be getting tired, the Master would somehow seem to know and he would send refreshments or come round in person. The Master also had a wonderful habit of being able to come around just as things were going wrong or we were getting stressed. He wanted us to aspire for perfection, true, but often speed was an important aspect of the Master's perfection."

"Now, this is my personal understanding of the Master's methods. When we aim for absolute physical perfection, the mind can feel it needs to plan, evaluate and ponder how to proceed. This brings our mental calculation and insecurity into the project. But, the Master never gave time for long, relaxed preparation – there was certainly no time to form a committee! Sometimes we were working so fast – we were just working on intuition, hoping it would all work out. I feel the Master valued most the consciousness we were in. If we are 100% committed, there is no time for hesitation and debate – you just get into the flow. In this state, the Master could work in and through you more easily. You have to bear in mind, Peter, that I didn't hear the Master say this directly – it is just my understanding."

Bahir interjected: "So you see, Peter. I'm not the only one who has a little bit of philosophy! But, it is very inspiring to hear Chetan share this reflection. It reminds me of a story – one of the rare occasions where I was actually involved in physical work for the Master. To be honest, I've always tried to avoid manual labour. But once I was visiting the Ashram café and Virat comes in a panic and says, 'Hey, I need some help – the Master needs his wall fixing right now.'

"Well, I had just ordered a very nice meal, so I try to look invisible, hoping Virat will pick someone else. But, at the same time my conscience starts to prick me. The Master needs something done straight away, but here I was – wanting to finish my eggs and sausages! I cringe about it now."

"Anyway there is no one else, and Virat asks me in a very nice way – it is impossible to say no. To be honest, when I see his face, I don't dare ask if he would mind waiting five minutes for me to finish my breakfast!"

"I go with him straight to the Master's outbuilding. It's hard physical work and the first hour is really tough. I'm still thinking about my breakfast and have mixed feelings about being there. I keep saying to myself it's a great honour to be working on the Master's wall, but my stomach is still rumbling with disapproval! As a result, I make a few mistakes and Virat gets frustrated, which he nicely shares with me. But, somehow I don't get affected – I feel his bark is worse than his bite. I also try to empathise with his situation – here he is trying to please his Master and I'm not 100% behind the project."

"Fortunately, at this point, some other disciples bring some snacks and refreshments. It fills something of the void left by breakfast and my stomach is pacified. After that short break, I really start to get into the flow. I stop thinking about whether I have better things to do, but just commit 100%. Then it starts to become enjoyable – digging holes in the ground is not my thing, but working for the Master was a great joy and satisfaction that day. Virat is much happier because he now sees the job is going well. He promises me that when we finish, he will take me out for a curry; this further picks up my spirits! The job goes well and, with a tremendous sense of satisfaction, we finish around 7pm. Just as we finish, the Master comes to inspect. As I remember, the Master said: 'This is an excellent job, Virat. I'm very grateful you have done such a good job.'"

"I'm tired but poised. In this state, I have no expectation or demands on the Master - just a sense of satisfaction. The Master says nothing to me, but gives a powerful smile of appreciation, which goes straight to my heart. It is a smile that is worth innumerable words. Now I'm thinking to myself: what a marvellous day! What an honour and privilege to work for the Master. If I had finished my eggs and then tried to meditate for four hours, would my consciousness be as elevated as this?

Almost certainly not!"

"But as the Master is walking away, he stops, turns around and comes back. 'Virat, I would be very grateful if perhaps tomorrow you could come back and fix the steps behind the back door, there is a loose tile.'

'Yes, Master,' says Virat.

"I don't mind. I'm sure tomorrow Virat will find his more usual workers – more skilled than me. The Master leaves and we get inside Virat's van. Now, I'm thinking we are going to the restaurant, but we stop at Virat's house and he dashes in to get some more tools. Then I realise we are driving back to the Master's compound. I say to Virat, 'I thought we were going to the curry house!' In an annoyed tone, Virat says, 'Didn't you hear the Master? He says he wanted his step at the back door to be fixed.'

"So I replied – with what I though was impeccable logic – 'But the Master said we can do it tomorrow'. Virat exploded in his own inimitable and endearing way, 'Heavens above, dear boy. Have you really been a disciple for fifteen years? When the Master asks us to do something, he means we should do it straightaway. The curry can wait, let us get this job done first.'"

"Well, I was amazed – both inspired by Virat's devotion and disappointed my stomach would have to be patient yet again!"

"After a few minutes, Virat softened and opened a box from his van full of delicious cakes. 'Emergency rations, Bahir. Always come in handy!' Virat still looked serious and stern, but if I nursed any resentment, it disappeared with the cake!"

"Well it turned out we fixed the step, and I got a real buzz from working late into the night. We did finally get a good curry, and my stomach was pacified for a second time that day."

"What a day. I'll never forget. That was the beauty of being in the presence of the Master – you could learn so much in a single day!"

# Coming to the spiritual life

"Peter, why should the old men do all the talking? Perhaps you could say how you came to the spiritual life?"

Peter replied: "Well in my student days I thought I could change the world through politics. I enjoyed taking controversial opinions and lecturing people on what I thought were the political truths. I would get involved in polemics with anyone who would listen or who was foolish enough to disagree. But, there was no peace in this subtle feeling of self-righteousness - just an inner anger and frustration that was eating me from inside. Then I had a big argument with a good friend, which left us polarised, and I thought: this is ridiculous, who cares who is right? So I stopped arguing. For a time, I gave up watching the news and reading endless things online because I felt so disgusted with it all."

"With this mindset, I was able to break out of my usual limited horizons, and I picked up a book on spirituality. It gave me a different perspective. No longer was it about trying to change other people, but trying to love the world, and getting a little peace in my own life."

"Now in politics I was intense, so I transferred this intensity to spirituality. I travelled around the country reading books, visiting healers, buying crystals, Reiki, meditation – if anything promised a bit of enlightenment I would give it a go. It was an exciting time, and my layers of cynicism and anger started to peel away. But, juggling several paths and approaches left me with a feeling of confusion. I also soon realised you couldn't spend your way to enlightenment! One week I was trying one path, the next week something else, but I couldn't settle."

"After travelling all over the country, I found myself back in my town of birth. Walking past a shop, I was struck by a poster. It had the title 'Meditation', but what really caught my eye was the photo of our Master. It was a feeling that evoked a sense of remembrance – like touching something from a far distant memory that suddenly felt very real and living. Disciples later told me they had put posters there for several years. But, it was only at that particular time I noticed."

"I went to the lecture and immediately felt at home – there was something beautiful in the atmosphere. I can't remember what the person giving the class really said, but I received a lot from the meditation, even though I didn't find it easy. I felt from the photos and his books that our Master was absolutely genuine. I'm not sure if anyone said directly he was a realised soul – but that is what I inwardly felt. The more I came, the more joy I received. I realised that after a class, I was counting down the days until the next. I felt like a man reborn; and with this new feeling of joy, my life started to change with unexpected rapidity. Former habits lost their lustre; I could no longer waste an evening having a few drinks and talking about the revolution. I wanted to go back home and try to meditate; the real revolution was going on in my mind and heart. I started to spend time just walking in nature. I never realised there was such a beautiful park, not one mile from where I lived. The park was the same as before, but now I was seeing in a new light."

"So that was it really; it helped to meet the other members of the Ashram who were very welcoming, and the community of like-minded people was inviting. My journey of meditation and spirituality had left me disconnected from my old life, and to a large degree my old friends. In a way, I was ready to press the reset button and start again. The only thing missing was the symbolic immersion in water!"

"Well, myself and Bahir can always arrange for you to be immersed in a lot of water," joked Chetan. Peter smiled.

"So how did you find it when you joined the main Ashram?"

asked Bahir.

"Well, it was really great. I must admit, at first, it felt like a big step and I wondered whether I was really ready for it. But once I actually joined and became a fully-fledged member, I knew I was choosing a life that had a real meaning and satisfaction. My early insecurities soon faded and I felt very welcomed."

Chetan added: "Well, of course, Peter, when you've been on the path as long as myself, it's always great to see young people with fresh enthusiasm and aspiration join. It provides a real shot in the arm for those who are keen to see the Master's legacy continue. And we don't just mean all that heavy lifting you do in the Ashram Press."

Peter smiled. "Well, there are certainly plenty of opportunities for selfless-service! People are never short of offering me opportunities in that department."

Bahir smiled and interjected, "Yes Peter, but just remember, you have it easy. When I was a new disciple all those 60 years ago, we would get up at 5 in the morning for a one-hour meditation, an early morning race, a bit of selfless service – and all before breakfast!"

Chetan leaned forward and added: "Yes Bahir, but I have to say, you don't know how lucky you were. When I joined the ashram – 10 years before you did – we would be getting up at 4.00am, two-hour meditation, and that was all after an evening function which ended in the small hours of the morning. The Master had unbounded energy and intensity in those early years. I don't know how we kept up, but we did."

Bahir laughed: "Yes, every year we manage to remember more epic meditations and intensity."

Chetan nodded: "Yes, self-transcendence in the recollection world. Anyway, we're interrupting poor Peter."

"No, not at all. I enjoy hearing any humorous recollections – even those where I wonder whether you may be exaggerating a little. One more thing I want to share, when I joined the path, I read about beautiful and lofty spiritual experiences of other seekers and spiritual Masters. But in my case – nothing. True, I was getting joy and having good meditations, but nothing special seemed to happen. And the harder I tried, the further away I seemed to get."

"Now I read in one of the Master's books about spiritual experiences. He wrote a spiritual experience is something that lifts up our consciousness. As the Master states, is not the real miracle being able to raise the human consciousness? If we feel goodwill towards the world rather than anger and frustration, is this not a spiritual experience? From reading this, I understood I had received a most significant and durable spiritual experience. But, at the same time, I still desired a little more!"

"Anyway, as the months went by, this desire faded a little from my mind, and I concentrated on following the spiritual life of meditation and selfless service."

"One time we were holding a meditation class just for one lone seeker. There were four of us from the Ashram and this old lady; to be honest, I don't know if she quite understood the Master's philosophy. So you begin to wonder whether it is worth your time, but then in the meditation - something happens – I do nothing special myself – but an external force seemed to lift me beyond the mind, and my consciousness is transformed. I'm overwhelmed with a sense of peace – not just a sense of calm and silence, but a peace that seems to embrace the whole world. I only wanted to share without distinction or judgement. It belonged to everyone and I felt a oneness with all of humanity."

"It did not feel like a personal achievement – more like remembering something long forgotten, remembering who I really was. And in this state it felt absurd I had ever forgotten who I really was – this self for which love and peace were as natural and imminent as breathing. In this consciousness, everything of the world – name, fame, wealth – all faded into insignificance by comparison. It was like waking from a grey and dreary world to remember how beautiful and joyful God's Creation really is. If only that meditation would last!"

"But, of course, it didn't last. Yet, even as it faded from the immediacy of the present, it left a reassuring afterglow – the imperceptible feeling that whatever suffering we go through, ultimately we would return to our source of Infinite Light."

Bahir and Chetan remained unusually silent. There was none of the usual joking, but an effortless and comfortable silence filled the room.

After a while, Chetan gently spoke.

"It reminded me of a time the Master was offering his sympathetic oneness with our daily challenges, but at the same time he seemed to soar far above these mundane difficulties. With the confidence and poise of his deepest realisation, he hinted our human dramas were no more than passing scenes of a dream. Far from being a universe of injustice, in everything he saw the invisible touch of God leading inexorably and mysteriously towards the Goal. Our deepest fears and gravest challenges are all but part of the Cosmic Game. And there would come a time when we would understand why everything had to be as it is."

"The Master smiled and gently said, 'In the sweep of Eternity, a human incarnation of 80 years is like a blink of the Supreme's Eye. To us on earth, how much we can suffer from day to day. But enjoy this human life while you can; you will soon enough have Eternity to commune with God and experience the infinite ecstasy of the Beyond.'"

"Through my Master's eye I felt I saw the tiniest reflection of this Celestial world, but even this tiny glimpse was enough for crusty layers of limited and proud beliefs to peel from my eyes. For an exhilarating second I knew my Master had already done everything for us. It was for us to stay the course and enjoy the journey."

There was a pause and Peter said, "That is so beautiful."

Chetan said, "Yes, with old age my memory fades, so what can you trust? It was a very rare insight; the Master was mostly concerned with the practical spirituality. But, always treasure your experience of peace, and try reading the Master's loftiest poems, because if you can read beyond the words, you can get a glimpse of that unearthly ecstasy. In his poetry, everything from our daily struggles to the highest realisation is there in seed form."

"Alas, liberation can still seem such a long way off." Peter said.

"Yes you're right, and as our Master said, we should not try to get our Master's degree, while we are still learning the ABCs of the spiritual life. But while we should not sit around thinking of our God-realisation, it is helpful and inspiring to at least remember our ultimate goal will more than compensate for any seeming sacrifices we may be making in this life of spiritual discipline."

# Technology

Peter asked Bahir, "Is it really true you grew up in a time without computers, smartphones and the internet?"

"Yes! See this is the proof of how old I am! When I was a child, if you wanted to speak to a friend, you might ring the one telephone shared by the whole house. Alternatively, you might just go round to their house and knock on their door to see if they were in! When our Ashrams were established by our Master, the smart-computer was a thing of science fiction. Everything would be organised and managed by phone, letters and meeting in person. Disciples think modern technology is absolutely indispensable – and maybe they are right – but at the same time, we thrived in that era."

Peter smiled and shook his head in disbelief. "So do you think we were better off then or now?"

"Our Master once said that science is offering to humanity the potential to have more leisure time for prayer and meditation. In the old days, monks would spend two years writing out the Bible by hand. Now we can publish a book with the click of a button. Those old Bibles were unimaginable works of devotion, literature and art, but who wants to go back to the old technology? If you can fly to Rome in one hour, why take the paddle-boat which takes two weeks?"

"However, just because science offers us more leisure time, it doesn't mean we always choose to avail ourselves of the opportunity. The problem is that when we get this extra free time, how do we use it? Do we use it for meditation and enjoying nature or do we spend our free-time surfing the internet and getting addicted to our smartphones? Technology can give us more time, but if we feel obliged to check our smart-computer every ten minutes, technology is not giving us freedom, but taking it away." Every year for the past 60 years, my New Year's Resolution has been the same – try to stop wasting time checking my computers and spend more time speaking to people rather than sending messages. Good resolutions is the easy part, but technology is designed to be addictive – so what has happened? We have forgotten how to enjoy a simpler approach to life."

Peter added: "But, I find technology is a good way to keep in touch with friends from abroad. I like to hear what they are up to."

"True, technology has reduced geographical boundaries, and in this sense you could say it has played a role in showing we can move closer towards a oneness-world. If we can speak to our friends on the other side of the world, how much inspiration we can get. But on the other hand, sometimes when you meet people in a social context, quite a few are constantly checking their smart-computers – even mid-conversation. When I see this, I worry we have lost the ability to switch off and be in the moment. In the old days, we would go to a restaurant and have a good time telling stories and jokes. Now, we go to the restaurant and people take photos of what they are eating so that their plates of food can be admired around the world. You can't escape! In this case, far from giving us a deeper connection, technology is making our social connections more superficial. When we speak to someone and they almost unconsciously, instinctively reach for their smart-computer, we wonder if they are fully present."

"Peter, as you know, I'm an old man, so I feel free to say these things. We old men like to speak our mind; whether this is a good thing or not, God alone knows! But, I worry we can all be too easily caught in the grip of technology. Computers, smartphones, internet can push us towards the superficial and away from the psychic heart and intuition. Technology gives us some benefits, true. But for the spiritual seeker, it is a double-sided coin."

Peter replied, "There is an increased awareness of these problems. Even in secular society, everyone is trying some kind of digital detox."

"This is good," replied Bahir. "But as spiritual seekers, we shouldn't just be following society, we should be the pathfinders of a new reality. It is not powerful technology which is going to bring down the Master's light - it is the cultivation of the heart and the intuitive faculties. If we are immersed in the digital screen, we are slowly suffocating our divine possibilities."

"People have to follow their inner intuition and work out how they want to get by in this modern world. But, I do secretly wonder - what our Master would say at the way everything has developed; I have a theory, but I wouldn't dare say - even to you! Peter, you're a good chap so I can speak freely. I wouldn't say this to everyone. But, I sometimes feel that if disciples really wanted to accelerate their spiritual progress, they would be best to throw their smartcomputer into the river!"

Peter smiled and replied: "On the one hand, I realise how it easy it is to use technlogy too much. But, at the same time, if I threw my smart-computer in the lake, I don't think I could survive in this world. You do realise you can't get on a plane without one these days?"

Bahir smiled. "Yes! I talk all about technology, but how did I make a living? I would say technology can give a benefit for humanity. But, it also requires a degree of self-discipline to make technology work for us, and avoid becoming slaves of technology ourselves."

"Peter, I am caught between two worlds. On the one hand, I

am praying that my next incarnation will be a technology-free world, where it is all heart, intuition and simplicity. But, at the same time, I quite enjoy the convenience of some modern technology – I definitely don't want to go back in time to the medieval ages, spending my life growing turnips by hand!"

"But, it's not my concern anymore, I am not long for this world. At least, I don't think you need a smart-computer to enter Heaven!"

# Parents and the spiritual life

There was a knock at the door. Peter spoke up, "Let me guess, another disciple, even older than you two!"

A giant of a man, with silver hair, entered the room and the three disciples burst into laughter.

Abhik was bemused but unruffled; he smiled and took a seat, stretching his huge feet towards the fire. As the laughter died down, Abhik spoke. "Well I'm very happy my arrival has caused so much joy."

Bahir said, "I'm sorry Abhik. It seems today young Peter is getting to meet all the Master's octogenarian disciples. Now Peter, I can promise you – Abhik is absolutely the oldest living direct disciple of the Master."

"Yes, but he is still more physically active and healthy than many of us who are 50 years his junior," added Chetan.

Peter asked the newcomer, "What is the secret of your good health?"

"Good health? Well looks can be deceptive. You don't get to be 95 years old without picking up your fair share of aches and pains. But our Master took a very practical and common sense attitude to health. As you know, he was vegetarian and advocated abstaining from intoxicating substances like drugs and alcohol. I feel that if I had kept the lifestyle of my youth, many decades ago I would have entered an early grave just like some of my friends from those hippy days of drugs and hedonism."

"When I joined my Master's Path, at first my parents were dead against it. They hoped I would become something respectable like a doctor or lawyer. The idea of following an Indian Guru was well outside their worldview."

"At first it was difficult because we had a mutual lack of understanding. On the one hand, my mother started to see some positive changes. She was relieved to see the end of my hippy lifestyle – out went the drugs, long hair and living in a filthy commune. But, on the other hand, she couldn't understand why I took a low-paid job working in the Ashram shop. She would say, 'For 15 years we have paid for your education, and now how are you using it? To sell incense and candles?' The truth is I felt great happiness in this new simple lifestyle. Although it did not make me outwardly rich, it gave an inner fulfillment. The problem is that when my mother's friends were showing off about the highly paid and prestigious professions of their children, my inner happiness was very poor currency in that artificial world of social climbing."

"Anyway, despite this little friction, my Master told me to persevere in keeping good relations with my parents. He said, 'Don't try to convert or explain. But also don't surrender your spiritual life to try and pacify their outer wishes.' So this is what I did and, over the years, I felt my parents started to inwardly appreciate my general happiness and relatively peaceful demeanour. To my greatest surprise, they even began expressing tentative interest in the spiritual life. So I asked my Master if they could come to one function and meet him in person. The Master said 'yes' and so they came. I have to say the Master melted their heart in a way that far exceeded my expectations. But, the funny thing is, at the time I was really quite nervous. When I brought my parents to the function, what did the Master do? Well, he holds an intense walking meditation and gives a serious talk. All this is hard to explain and I'm wondering what my parents will be thinking. With my parents, I always kept the spiritual life very general and vague. But, with his usual imperturbable poise, the Master just did his own thing!"

"But, then towards the end of the evening, the Master 'remembers' and he says to me, 'Abhik, why didn't you tell me your parents are here, good boy?' The Master doesn't wait for me to answer but starts speaking to my parents. And to my astonishment the Master says, 'I am very proud of your Abhik. Don't tell him because it will go to his head, but I'm very grateful to you for bringing into the world such a nice soul.' Well, it made a very nice change from the scoldings I usually received from the Master! And then the Master begins a nice conversation – with my parents asking spiritual questions, and the Master answering in his own loving and imitable way. In our house we don't mention the world 'God'. God doesn't exist in our lexicology. But, the Master spoke about God with such effortless confidence and close familiarity – you felt it was as natural as the existence of the sun."

"Now later that evening, my parents said very nice things about my Master and our Path. I think it was something their heart and soul had felt since the very first day but now their minds were convinced too. But, even if they hadn't said anything, I could tell from their faces, they understood our Path and had received a lot."

"Now shortly after my parents' outer acceptance, the Master asks me to change jobs, and I find myself working in an international environment of high-ranking officials. Through the Master's grace, over the next few decades, I am sometimes the instrument for the Master meeting some influential world figures. So, from where to where? My parents now have their spiritual son meeting all these big shots and they can show off these photos to their friends!"

"Now Peter, what was your question again?" Abhik laughed to himself but didn't give Peter time to answer. He answered his own rhetorical question.

"Why have I lived a long time? Well, it's not because I preserve life-energy by remaining silent!"

"Our Master just encouraged a balanced lifestyle – especially to keep the body fit and active. Even when the Master was weighed down by physical ailments in the evening of his life, how hard he endeavoured to keep fit. This has been a great example and inspiration in my own 'retirement years'. Even now that I'm 95 years old, I still do what I can."

"And you do a better job than we who are merely 70 years old." added Chetan.

"About diet the Master advocated vegetarianism, but apart from that he was not so specific. I think he was wary of faddy diets, which can make the practitioner obsessed with food. But, at the same time, as I get older I find cutting down on processed foods and sugar has made it easier to absorb the natural goodness of food."

"So Peter, do you want to live until you're 100 years old?"

"Well Abhik, you are a tremendous inspiration – but to be honest I'm struggling to get through my 20s, let alone my 100s!

"Yes, don't worry about old age. It will come soon enough!"

# Imperfect disciples

Peter asked, "How do you deal with a situation when there is a difference of opinion between disciples working on a project?" asked Peter.

Abhik remarked, "Well that is a good question, and of course there are different ways to answer!"

Bahir jumped in, "For example, me and Chetan often had disagreements about the best way to proceed. And so we would sit down to talk – allowing us to express our respective viewpoints in a polite, constructive and harmonious manner and, after a certain period of time, we would eventually arrive at the mutually agreeable conclusion that I was right!"

Chetan laughed. "Yes, very true. But what Bahir never realised is that outwardly I would always agree with him. 'Yes, Bahir, let us do it your own way.' And then I would nicely go away and do it in my own way anyway!"

Bahir smiled and added: "Yes, in that way, we were both happy! Sometimes you have to be wise. There are different roads to Rome; you don't necessarily all have to travel on the same road, at the same speed. If people want to take their time admiring the scenery on the way, don't force them to travel at your speed as they will resent you, and you will suffer too. Of course, if you see someone travelling in completely the wrong direction, then if you have concern for your fellow disciples, you should say something."

Chetan added, "This is good advice, though it is also worth bearing in mind it can be safer and stronger to travel in a group. The Master established certain key projects for the Ashram – if you see something you feel that could be done better, don't just go away and do your own thing. Try to join and make the project stronger with a constructive and helpful attitude."

Bahir said: "One thing I should add is that if you are doing all the work, it does give you a degree of say. Often in the Ashram, people get inspired to come up with ideas and suggestions. But, ideas are 'ten a penny'. The best ideas are usually those where the person with the idea is also willing to lead from the front and work very hard to get the project going. If people see a project is inspiring and also is coming from the right motivation, then naturally it will inspire others to join. But, if you sit in a café and tell people it would be good idea to go out and dig drainage ditches, well, good luck in getting people to listen!"

Abhik leaned forward and said, "Although we joke a little, the Master did speak on this issue. The Master said something to the effect, 'When you work on a project, your inner harmony is more important than the outer result. Suppose you see one way of proceeding, but my leader in that field is doing it another way. Then – as long as they are not doing something wrong or going against the spirit of my path – please offer your selfless service according to that way. Suppose you can think of a more efficient method – if it breaks the spirit of harmony, at that time I do not want your cleverness and efficiency. If disciples can work in a spirit of humility, detachment and cheerfulness, this in itself is a real achievement and real manifestation.'"

"And what advice did the Master give to those who would be responsible for leading projects?" asked Peter.

Bahir replied, "The Master said that those who lead a project must do so with great humility. A leader is not someone who lords it over other people, but someone who sets a good example and is encouraging of other people. Also, they should never feel that they are the real leader. Our only real leader is the Supreme himself."

Abhik added, "I once heard the Master say, 'A leader should be a ladder.' In other words a leader should help people to come to the fore and feel valued in making progress."

Chetan said, "Often the people who find themselves in roles of leaders are those who don't particularly want to be there. Also, if you want to be a good leader, it is important to also be able to follow too. If you see things from both sides, it gives you a wider understanding."

"What about since the Master's physical passing? How do you know the right thing to do?" asked Peter.

Bahir said, "Well, in some respects it can be challenging. After the Master's passing, we realised how fortunate we were to have a realised soul guide us on the physical plane in so many small details. Sometimes the Master's attention to detail was incredible, and you always had the confidence that the Master would be saying the right thing. But now we don't have that luxury – instead we have to work harder on cultivating our prayer capacity and our meditation capacity. As you know, Abhik, Chetan and myself are involved in one aspect of the Master's service to the world. If someone has a new idea and we all agree, then that is fine. However, if one of us had inner doubts, our Master told us we should wait. As you know, the Master valued speed. But, speed is not much good if you're heading in the wrong direction! It is always important to have the right foundations – otherwise the project will be on shaky ground and can even cause damage if it comes crashing to the ground. If one person feels something is not right, it is better to be patient, observe and meditate on the question."

Chetan continued, "The Master says that if a sincere devotee is trying to do the right thing, God will definitely find a way to try and help them. The thing we have to bear in mind is that when it comes to listening to God's advice, we often have very poor hearing. The problem is our own mind, vital and emotions make so much noise, they often drown out the still inner voice within. That is why we have to be patient and really try to go deep within to find the answer."

Bahir took up the conversation, "Yes, that is very good advice, and it also helps to consider your own motives. If your way happens to please your ego and sense of self-aggrandisement, then it becomes even more important to proceed with caution. Sometimes it is really hard to know what to do. But, if you have a calm, patient attitude, seemingly intractable problems can lead to unexpected solutions."

"Also, even if outwardly it is not all plain-sailing, if we are sincerely trying to do the right thing, then we feel an inner peace – no matter what is happening outwardly."

Peter asked: "How do you avoid minor personality conflicts and manage to deal with the imperfections of other disciples?"

"Firstly, did the Master have any disciple who was even close to being a perfect instrument? This is the nature of the world – imperfection rules. If we wait for the perfect disciple to help us, we will not budge an inch. The Master himself was always working with imperfect instruments. How often he had difficulties because of disciples' imperfections – just read the Master's own illumining stories! But, if we were living with the Master seven days a week for year after year, would we be able to maintain perfection? So we need a degree of tolerance – we can't expect perfection in others, when we don't have it in ourselves."

Abhik said, "I remember when I was a new disciple so many years ago. One disciple was physically very close to the Master – he performed many daily tasks for him. But, when I first met this disciple, I was quite surprised – if not shocked. How many bad qualities did he have! He looked scruffy, had a quick temper and said words that were quite frankly not in my vocabulary! I thought to myself, 'How can the Master keep such a roguish character so close to him?' But then, maybe a year or two later, for some reason I got up at 4 in the morning – and who do I see emptying the garbage at this unearthly hour? Yes, that so called roguish disciple – who was actually putting us all to shame. How many of us would volunteer for that difficult job, which comes with no recognition, yet we all take for granted? So I felt humbled because here I was judging a disciple by their vocabulary – but hidden underneath the rough exterior was extraordinary selflessness."

"So we have to be careful to avoid too much judgement and criticism of other disciples, because otherwise we will miss their good qualities – qualities we may not even have ourselves."

# Was life easier in the past?

Peter spoke to Abhik, "Earlier we were having a nice conversation with Bahir about how life was different 80 years ago. Do you feel the spiritual life was easier 80 years ago when the Master was in the physical?

Abhik replied, "I don't know if the spiritual life was ever easy – and I don't think it will ever get any easier in the future! But, it is a good question and I remember many years ago somebody asked the Master a similar question. They asked: is it easier to aspire now or 200 years ago?"

"The Master said that although he deeply appreciates the scientific development of the world, in some regards it has made the spiritual life more difficult. In the modern life, we can give the mind so much food. All the time we are getting information; it is like standing under a waterfall trying to get a glass of water. We give the mind so much but human nature always wants to give the mind even more. However, if we overfeed the mind to excess, we starve the heart; our heart needs a very different kind of food."

"The outer wealth adds nothing to the heart, and craving for too many possessions can diminish the psychic part of ourself. Also, the Master said another challenge of modern life is that when we do anything, we often want the whole world to know. There is a constant craving for recognition and attention. And I have to say the Master gave this talk before the world of social media. Perhaps he saw something of the future when he said this."

Bahir spoke up, "It reminds me of a teaching of our Master. He said, 'Try to see what you can do for my Mission without any recognition. If you can serve without expectation of reward or recognition, it is the highest selfless service.'"

"Well that reminds me of a story," began Chetan.

"For two weeks, I worked tirelessly on a project. Every day from dawn to dusk I worked on the Master's spiritual festival. We had fun, but service to the Master came first. In all honesty, I felt privileged to serve. The service was its own reward."

"The event was a great success and afterward the Master heaped praise – not on me, but a dear friend. Well, when I say dear friend, I should explain! While we worked from dawn to dusk, my friend sat in a café or played tennis, occasionally telling us what to do! So when the Master started praising him to the sky, my ego leapt forward. Inwardly I was shouting inside: 'Hey, Master, what about me!'"

"I knew my friend did virtually nothing – but he was getting all the praise. As a result, I was in a bad mood, and as I walked past my Master, he averted his eyes and would not even give me a smile of recognition. I was a bit put out to say the least. So I tried to meditate on this issue; I felt the Master was trying to teach me detachment. For two weeks, I had been in a great consciousness working for the Master – why should I become depressed just because he praised someone else? So I consciously remembered the feeling of joy from the past two weeks. It helped a lot – though I realised the philosophy of surrender and detachment could be much harder in reality than theory!"

"Now two days later my good friend comes to me and says, "Chetan, I have to admit I was a bit embarrassed when the Master was praising me to the skies. I played more tennis than I worked on the project. My conscience was pricked when the Master gave me all the praise but you did all the work. So the next day, I sent the Master a note saying who had really done all the work. In reply the Master said, 'Yes. I already knew.'"

"I find this fascinating because by praising the wrong person, look how the Master illumined two people at once. The Master was able to gently scold my friend for not doing any work, and to me he taught the value of selflessness and not the outer praise. When I heard about the note, I immediately forgave my friend – he is maybe lazy but at least he is sincere!"

Abhik added, "Yes, that is a great story. We all have experiences like that – who does not feel under-appreciated at some time? One thing I should add: we should not go to the other extreme and hold back good news. When I was a new disciple, I got a very good article about our path in a newspaper. And I thought I shouldn't brag but try to be humble, so I didn't tell."

"But of course, the Master found out and he asked, 'Abhik, why did you not share the good news?' And I was silent because I didn't know what to say. But, the Master knew without words and he spoke to all the disciples. 'Real humility lies in giving joy to other people. Humility is not hiding in a corner; that is often the false modesty, and our motives are not divine. So if you have good news, feel the value of sharing. If you speak to your brother and sister disciples, you will feel it is a deeper achievement. If any of my disciples achieves something good, immediately I feel my oneness and claim it as my own. Equally, if by the Grace of God, I am able to achieve something in the outer world, I want my disciples to feel their oneness with me. If there is oneness, there is no room for jealousy and pride. So, Abhik, this is a very good article, but next time, please let us know."

Chetan said: "Bahir it is an interesting talk that you remember, but on another occasion the Master answered slightly differently. Someone asked about the golden age of spirituality. And the Master replied, 'What Golden Age of Spirituality?' The Master said it is a mistake to assume in the past people were much more spiritual, just because they were poor. We can romanticise the past, but the past has similar obstacles to the present – those recurring aspects of human nature: pride, ego and ignorance. In the future, we will have these same obstacles within our nature too."

Peter asked, "Would the Master often answer questions in different ways?"

"Well, yes and no," said Abhik with a smile.

"If you read through the Master's writings you will see a wonderful thread of the loftiest spirituality. But, the Master was not constrained by an artificial consistency. Spirituality is not two-dimensional but multilayered. Also, it would depend who asked the question. If a beginner asked the Master, 'How long should I meditate for?' the Master might say, '5 minutes.' To a new disciple, the Master might say, 'Try meditating for 20 minutes in the morning and evening.' To an experienced disciple he might say, 'Please try meditating for two hours a day.'

Bahir broke in, "Once I was with a group of disciples and the Master said to us, if you are very good disciples, you can please try to meditate for at least eight hours a day."

"Eight hours!" exclaimed Chetan. "I never heard that."

"Why, how long do you meditate for Chetan?" asked Bahir.

"Well, about eight minutes in the morning and eight minutes in the evening."

"That's very good. You're an excellent disciple. You're nearly 50% of the way there!"

Everybody laughed. Peter asked, "So how long should I actually meditate for?"

Abhik responded, "The real answer is that it depends. It is not the duration of the meditation, but the quality. If you sit for four hours in the lotus posture but your mind is full of useless, impure thoughts – well, as one Master said, 'You might be better off going to play football.' But, if you meditate for 30 minutes and you feel there is an inner stillness, an inner awakening, then try to extend your meditation. If you feel joy in the heart, but you stop because there is something on television, you are missing out on a divine opportunity."

Bahir added, "It also depends on where you are. When we meditate in the main Ashram Hall, there is a greater intensity, purity and awareness of the Master's consciousness. In that exalted environment I find time can fly by and I'm surprised at my capacity to meditate, but when I go home, it's another story."

"Also, everybody is different," said Chetan. "I still think old Bahir was a monk. Definitely no comedian!" His nature is drawn to meditation, but to me the spiritual life has been about service and offering the Master's music to the world at large. I feel that when I can offer the Master's soulful songs, I receive much more than sitting at home in meditation."

Bahir said: "Actually this conversation brings to mind another story that I heard from my old friend Bodhi. As a new disciple, he was very keen to meditate. Early morning it was - meditation, breakfast, and then a second post-breakfast meditation."

"I'm the other way around - two breakfasts and one meditation!" said Chetan.

"Yes, that is more likely! Anyway Bodhi was walking back from breakfast when he met the Master on the street, and the Master stopped Bodhi and asked 'Where are you going?' And then, with a certain amount of pride, Bodhi replied 'Well, I'm going for my second post-breakfast meditation.' But, the Master wasn't impressed with that, and he replied to Bodhi. 'No, I'd like you to come and work for me in the gardens. One morning meditation is sufficient.'

"Bodhi was of course happy to go and work for the Master. But, the story didn't end there. A couple of months later, Bodhi was walking along the street at ten minutes past five in the morning. Again he bumped into the Master and again the Master asked Bodhi 'Where are you going?' With a certain amount of pride, Bodhi replied 'I'm going to the printing press to work on your new book.' But, again the Master wasn't impressed and he asked Bodhi 'what time did you get up to meditate?' And Bodhi replied with a hint of embarassment 'Er, about five minutes ago Master.' The Master gave an exasperated smile and said to Bodhi: 'The problem is that you always go to extremes. 'I don't want you to be meditating during the working day. But, equally, I don't want you to have just a perfunctory meditation in the morning. Even if you are working on my special projects, don't neglect your morning meditation. The spiritual life needs balance Bodhi.'

Abhik smiled and added, "If you asked the Master whether you should meditate more, the Master would also use his inner vision to give the answer the person needed. If he saw the person had spiritual capacity, but was wasting their life in idle pursuits, he would be likely to answer in a way that encouraged them to meditate for longer. However, if he saw that a disciple was secretly proud because they were meditating for a long-time, the Master may say something completely different. But, you don't have to worry – if you read all the Master's writings on meditation and sincerely try to do the right thing, he will definitely inwardly guide you."

# Giving meditation classes

Peter and Bahir were joined by Alex.

"Well, I've been doing a lot talking this afternoon," said Bahir. "But whilst I relive the old days – going on and on – you and Peter are actually going out into the world to share the Master's philosophy."

Peter replied, "That's very kind. But, when I'm 78 years old, I will definitely be living on my former glories too! It's true the Master valued action, but these stories are not idle talk or gossip; they are real treasures. When I hear these stories about the Master, I feel surcharged with aspiration and gratitude to be following this spiritual path. You tell stories of being with the Master in the physical, but when I hear them, I feel them as my own. It is like I was there with the Master – going through the same mistakes, triumphs and struggles. There is part of me wishing I was born 100 years ago, but on the other hand, I feel that everything of the Master has an immediacy and connection with the present."

Bahir said, "That is absolutely right, the Master always encouraged us to feel oneness with his achievements and experiences. If we live in the heart, we are not constrained by time and space."

Bahir turned to Alex and said, "It's good to see you, Alex. I hear you were giving a meditation course in town recently. How did it go?"

"Well, public speaking is not my thing, but I think it went OK. I did a few nice meditation exercises, but – despite preparing a lot of material – I found that I quickly ran out of things to say, so my talk was quite limited."

"Excellent," said Bahir, laughing to himself. "Some of us give meditation classes for 50 years but, despite a lot of practise, we never manage to learn that art of running out of things to say. Silence is golden!"

Alex smiled. "True, meditation can best be understood in silence, but I would like to become a better speaker because people appreciate some explanation. Also when I came to the Ashram, I found Tom's classes quite humorous and light-hearted – this helped to relax the audience and make them more receptive."

"Yes, that is true, but I would say: don't worry at all. When I first gave classes, I had the same issue of running out of things to say. The only advice I would give is to be sincere; be yourself. Don't try to imitate others, but if you are sincere about the path, and the people feel something of the Master's light, they will be inspired to go straight to the source – this is not what you are saying, but the Master's meditation and the Master's books. Also, Tom is a really excellent class-giver – he has a natural talent – but did you join the Master's path because he told a few half-baked jokes that he got from me?"

"To be fair, Bahir, Tom does tell them a lot better!"

"Yes, I know!" said Bahir.

"What did the Master say about giving meditation classes, Bahir?" asked Alex.

"Well, I'm not entirely sure whether he gave any specific instructions. I always felt the Master was most concerned that we were just willing to offer classes and lectures in the first place. The Master was not concerned about whether we were great speakers or had immaculate preparation. No one becomes a real disciple of the Master because a lecturer is eloquent with words. It has to be from that inner connection, inner meditation and the soul's affinity to the Master's light and consciousness."

"I'll tell you a funny story. Many years ago when the Master's path was quite new, the idea of giving meditation classes or lectures wasn't very developed. In those days, people would become the Master's disciple through many different ways – such as just seeing him at a concert or meeting him in person. But anyway, an old friend Jahangir said that once he found out about the Master, he was really keen to find out more. So he found a contact address for a local Ashram centre and went around to their house. When he arrived, he was welcomed by an elderly gentleman, and Jahangir said he was interested in becoming the Master's disciple. Now this elderly gentleman was not really a class giver, so he invited Jahangir into a meditation room and invited him to meditate on a picture of the Master. Then this elderly gentleman said he had to pop out to run some errands and he would be back in a couple of hours. So Jahangir sat in this meditation room for two hours. He had a very good meditation and when the old gentleman came back, Jahangir said, 'Great. I'd like to apply to be a disciple of the Master! I feel something very special from this meditation.'"

"Now, I'm not saying that when you give a meditation class, you should leave your class to sit in silence for two hours while you go out and do your shopping. But this shows the potential that even if you don't say anything particularly profound, a real seeker can get fed from the Master in silence."

"That is very inspiring," said Peter. "Though if my first meditation class was sitting alone in a room for two hours, I don't know what I would have made of it. I think I may have run away! But, at the same time, one of the things that impressed me was meditating on the Master's picture. Also, I felt the other disciples had something of the Master's light – at least I was impressed with their bearing and selflessness."

Alex said, "Yes, that is why it is good if new disciples like Peter come along to our classes. Seekers pick up on their energy, inspiration and enthusiasm. It is not about sharing deep philosophy, but seekers can see the sincerity and devotion – even if they can't quite put their finger on it."

Alex added, "One thing I found helpful when giving classes was something old Brian told me several years ago: 'When giving classes, don't think in terms of getting new members of the Ashram. Just feel it is like an offering and allow people to take whatever they are ready to eat. Some people, when they go to a buffet, want to just take a small snack to fill a little gap. Some of us are much more hungry and want the full three-course meal. But, if you're not hungry, eloquent speeches won't make you want to eat."

Peter said, "Yes, but in my case, I went just for a smaller than the smallest snack. Then, when I had my first bite, it tasted really good – so I became greedy and wanted to eat a lot more!"

Bahir laughed. "Yes, the Master would often say that our inner hunger is the most important thing in the spiritual life. If we have the inner hunger, we don't have to worry about our meditation technique or our personal weaknesses. It is the inner hunger, the inner aspiration which will burn away these outer imperfections."

Peter asked. "Is there anything we can do to increase our inner hunger, our inner aspiration?"

Bahir answered, "This is an interesting question. When I was very young, I had a real taste for junk food. For every meal, I would eat chips, white bread and doughnuts. So naturally, this is what I craved. But once I got sick, so I tried a different diet of fresh fruits, vegetables and whole-grains. When I tried this diet, I found I cultivated very different tastes, my greed for the junk food diminished and my hunger for the more healthy food increased. In the spiritual life, we have to cultivate the right tastes. If we spend our time watching soap operas and going to bars and clubs, we will not be able to cultivate the taste for spiritual peace. But if we spend time with fellow spiritual travellers, then we will be nourished, and it will be much easier to be inspired about the spiritual life. Another spiritual Master said that the human mind is like blotting paper – it absorbs whatever it is exposed to. So we have to be careful what we dip the blotting paper – our mind – into. If we are surrounded by spiritual vibrations, then it becomes considerably easier and more natural to aspire. Peter, is there anything you would add from your own recent experience?"

"Well, I agree with what you say," replied Peter. "It is hard to enjoy the taste of sugar and salt at the same time. The problem is that if you are enjoying a real feast of sweetness, a salty dish confuses the taste buds. When I joined the spiritual life, I found I lost quite a few of my former attachments and habits. But, as they drifted away, I felt a sense of liberation. Then, once you get a taste of meditation and what it can bring, you really appreciate and would like to experience more. One thing I would add. I read in the Master's writings that if we have a good spiritual experience, we should remember it with gratitude. Also if we write it down, it will help us remember; then when we have low periods we can read what we have written and it will help bring the experience back. This was helpful for me. The first year or two, I felt I was absolutely flying, and I thought: it's only a matter of time before I enter into trance or something like that. But just as I was flying very high, my progress seemed to stop and I felt I went right back to where I started. Then I began doubting my own experiences, my own commitment to the spiritual life. But, when I re-read some of my notes from those early days of aspiration, it helped bring the feeling back to a reasonable degree and my doubts seemed entirely misplaced."


Alex said: "It's a good point. I can only say it is a very common experience that you share. The Master once said that quite often when we start the spiritual life, the Supreme gives us a most significant experience - to give us encouragement and show us the possibilities of a spiritual life. But, then we have to work hard to regain and then transcend this early experience."

Bahir smiled and said, "It also brings to my mind something the Master said. When we start the spiritual life, it can feel like a plane taking off. Because we are getting off the ground, the speed can feel very high – we are accelerating from zero to 100mph in a few seconds. However, once airborne it can feel like we are hardly moving, when actually we are cruising at 500mph – we are just not aware of how fast we are going. It can be like that in the spiritual life – it's not all beautiful experiences. Sometimes transforming our nature is hard work, but if we stick at it and stay on the plane, then we will make considerable progress. The only problem comes if we want to jump out because we feel we are not getting anywhere. Patience is a virtue – that is at least one thing I have learnt in the past 80 years!"

# Helping at the race

A few weeks later, the Ashram were promoting a local 10km running race in a local park. The race was being organised by Alex.

"Bahir, what are you doing here?" said Alex in a terse voice.

"I heard there was a job for an old man where I could sit down," said Bahir.

"O you've come to help!" said Alex. "That's really great, sorry I was thinking of many things at once just then. Well sitting down jobs are always very popular. But, I say the oldest gets first pick in terms of sitting jobs!"

"Yes. Thank you!" said Bahir. "At least in terms of numbers of years, there is at least one thing where I can claim top spot in the Ashram."

"It's a great honour you come and help at our local running race. I can hardly believe it!" said Alex.

"Well, it's good to get out of the house, my fellow retirees can hardly believe that I go out and help at a running race either. I think that they are maybe secretly a little jealous," said Bahir with a smile.

"How many people do you expect at tonight's race?" asked Bahir.

"I think around 150," replied Alex.

"Well, good luck. I shall sit here and make sure nobody goes off course."

"And if they do, Bahir, I'm relying on you to run after them and bring them back."

"Right you are. I used to be a good runner back in the last century. I'm sure the old magic is still in there somewhere. Now, I'll let you get on and concentrate on organising the race. If you're not careful, you will end up having to listen to all my running stories from the era of timing by hand and analogue clocks."

"What do you mean 'timing by hand'? ... Yes, let us catch up after the race is over, and I can start to relax a little."

[After the race]

"Well, that seemed to go well," said Bahir.

"Yes, fortunately, everything seemed to go quite smoothly and the runners seemed to enjoy and appreciate the race," said Alex.

"Well, you look as though a weight has been lifted off your shoulders," said Bahir.

"Yes. I've been organising races for 10 years, but there is always a sense of satisfaction mixed with relief when it all passes off smoothly," said Alex.

"It's also great to see a good turnout from the fellow Ashram members who come to help," said Bahir.

"Yes, we couldn't do it without a big turnout. It's really great to have so many helpers from the Ashram – from our very newest members to our very own vintage disciples."

Bahir smiled and said, "I wonder who you could mean by a vintage disciple? I don't think I've heard that term of endearment before."

"Yes. They say a good bottle of wine improves with age – the longer they are kept at the right temperature, the more they improve... Not that I would know anything about vintage wine, you have to remember!"

"O, Yes. I believe you Alex. But, I'm not sure this bottle of wine has always been kept at the right temperature. There's part of this bottle that has definitely seen better days. Sitting while helping is a great job!"

Alex smiled: "So, does this bring back memories of your own golden age of running?"

"Well, I'm not sure there was ever a golden age of running! I was very much one of the also-rans. Somebody has to make up the numbers!" said Bahir.

"Yes, that is true."

"But, whatever my speed, running gave a great joy and sense of achievement. As you know, the Master really valued running – it gives a dynamism and joy which is a great complement to the inner silence of meditation."

"What about organising races? How was that?" asked Alex.

"Well, I was involved in organising races for quite a few years. When I first joined the Ashram, I was not a little surprised to see this was part of our spiritual path. But, I soon realised why the Master encouraged us to organise these public races. They are a time when the Ashram can come together in working for a very positive and tangible offering to the public. The thing about our races is that we don't directly bring in our spiritual philosophy. But, it is there in an unstated and unspoken way – just by the spirit with which we offer the race. It shows to the general public that spirituality is not about retreating from the world, but following a normal life: a life that has a clear goal, dynamism, self-offering and cheerfulness. You can give a lecture on all this, but who wants to come and listen? As the Master said, 'Actions speak louder than words.' When we offer races, I think we are able to offer his philosophy through actions and not words."

"Yes," said Alex, "and one thing I like about the races is meeting the running community. We get a lot of inspiration from their involvement and participation. We are not trying to achieve anything in particular, but the Master is right that sport and races can bring out the best in humanity – because of the focus and opportunity for self-transcendence."

Bahir added: "The other thing I like about our races is that it is a very nice thing for members of the Ashram to participate in. Whatever is happening in our spiritual life, helping out at a race is an easy way to feel like an active member and have an opportunity to contribute something very positive. When I saw you before the race, one hundred percent, I emphasised and felt your pre-race nervous tension. In theory, meditation should give you perfect equanimity and detachment, but when it comes to organising a big race, well it definitely gives you an opportunity to try and practise this!"

Alex asked, "Are there any tips you would give for organising races?"

"Well, one story comes to mind. I had been organising races for 20 years without any major problems, and that particular year, it was really hard work getting approval from the national athletics body. Every year they bring in new forms, safety regulations and the like – never-ending transcendence in the bureaucracy world! I remember the days when you could literally turn up at a park and just put up a finish sign! Anyway, I digress. So for several weeks, it was back and forth, filling in the forms, dotting the i's, and crossing the t's. Whenever they raised a problem, I straightaway tried to address it. Finally, after all this hassle, we got our insurance and I felt a great relief. Now, there was one last thing to do, which was to inform the council. This was the easy part. It was literally a five or ten-minute job. But, because it was such an easy job, relaxation came in. I said to myself, 'Since it is so easy, I can do it anytime.' So I went to do some other tasks that I felt were more important."

"Every now and then, it would come to my mind to do this last job. But, I kept saying to myself, 'This is the easy part – I can do it anytime.' Anyway, suddenly I realised it was April and our races started in May. But, the council required two months notice! I had spent literally two months saying to myself, 'I can do this anytime, it is such an easy job!' But how quickly can time pass! I was really annoyed with myself and I had to go to the council and really plead with them to break their own rules and give us permission with just one month's notice. And I'm sure you know what councils are like with rules and regulations. So this 'easy' job proved to be very taxing, plus time-consuming! Fortunately, to my great relief, I got to speak to a very nice woman on the council who was friendly to our races, and we managed to break through the impenetrable inertia and mass of council regulations. I was most relieved our races were able to go ahead. But, it taught me a valuable lesson – 'Don't put off until tomorrow what you can do today.' Also, how much mental energy I wasted spending two months putting off the simple job. I learnt a valuable lesson. Never underestimate easy jobs!"

"Thank you for sharing that experience," said Alex. "I'm sure it is a good lesson for all of us. I know the feeling of relaxation and how dangerous that can be. In fact, hearing that reminds me I ought to go away and finish the results – before I spend the whole day listening to your golden stories from the past."

"Yes, you do the right thing," said Bahir. "It's no real relaxation when – in the back of your mind – you have things left unfinished. Just remember that by serving the Master through organising the races, you are really offering something very positive to the rest of the world. We cannot always know how our service affects other people – but, I do feel many are grateful for our races."

"Thank you, Bahir. Let us catch up when the race season is over!"

# Weekly meditations

"Hello, good to see you Peter," said Bahir.

"Yes, it's great to see you Bahir," replied Peter. "But, we really miss you – we haven't seen you at the Ashram meditations for quite a few weeks now."

Bahir replied: "In heart and soul I am there, but alas the body is getting left behind. I could come, but it would be a painful experience for me. I don't want to disturb with my coughing and spluttering. I feel the weekly meditation is not just about my own personal benefit. I feel it is more like contributing to the collective meditation – the team effort if you like. When I come, I want to add to the team's strength rather than take away."

"I have to say, for many years, I never missed our weekly meditations. Apart from illness or giving meditation lectures in other towns, I would always come. I remember one time – after going to every meeting for several years, I thought I had built up enough credits to deserve a week off. So I entered a running race, which was held at the same time as our main Thursday evening meditation. It was a race I had always wanted to do, but in the past I had felt I needed to 'sacrifice' the race and go to meditation instead. Now, can you guess what happened? The race got cancelled, so I made the meditation after all. Perhaps it was my bad luck, perhaps it was my good luck or perhaps it was somebody upstairs pulling a few strings. I can almost imagine my Master saying, 'So Bahir, you think you deserve a week off! Well, I have other ideas!' The funny thing is, after that experience, I lost the desire to miss meditation to go and do a race. Though it probably helped that I was starting to get slower as a runner!"

"How do you find our weekly meditations, Peter?"

"They are very good. I like the meditation and the singing, but I also find that just as valuable is the opportunity to spend time with disciples after the meditation and share some soup and tea. I feel very nourished from hearing about the activities of the Ashram around the world. Also, I love hearing stories about the Master and the spiritual life. That is why we miss you. You always have inspiring, humorous stories about the spiritual life. Sometimes we get a little – let us say – sidetracked, but when you're there, how effortlessly you can steer the conversation away from more contentious issues and back to spirituality or humorous anecdotes. I wish I had that capacity. When politics comes up, I want to start giving the lectures of my youth, and I have to literally bite my tongue."

"Peter, you are right. I often feel this time of relaxation after a meditation can be as important as the meditation itself. And it was like that with the Master. At functions we would have serious meditation – absolutely all soulfulness, all silence. But, after this meditation, the Master could easily bring forward a completely different quality of sweetness, innocence and joy. Sometimes the Master would say the magic words, 'Cock and Bull story', and everyone woke up because we knew the Master was going to share a juicy story from his early life, or perhaps recent experience. Sometimes the Master repeated stories, but that didn't matter at all. It wasn't the information, but listening to the Master's delightful retelling that gave you a real sense of closeness to the Master – we were at his feet, and we were basking in the reality he was creating from sharing his humorous and illumining experiences. The Master had so many aspects, but this aspect was one of my favourites because it is so immediately accessible – whatever consciousness you are in."

"Peter, I'm an old man so I can make a confession. Sometimes, in weekly meditations, my meditation itself is absolutely useless! But when Chetan and Abhik told us stories about the

Master, I felt a lot of joy, which more than compensated for any perceived inadequacy in meditation. Also, when I was a new disciple, I was shy, quiet and I used to admire the older disciples who could talk about spirituality in a way that was light, humorous and refreshing. How sincerely I admired the sterling qualities of some older disciples. Now the Master once said that if we sincerely appreciate the good qualities of other people, this is a very powerful force for bringing these qualities into our ourselves. We will not need to imitate, but we will find that within we also have these same qualities that we admire in other people. So you do absolutely the right thing to appreciate these qualities. Have patience and confidence, and you will see."

"Now, in another way, we are also sailing in the same boat. After meditation who wants to talk about politics? The Master said, 'One human opinion can divide the world.' This is true. My only consumption of politics comes from political satire, because I feel in satire there is more truth than you get from a newspaper. Well, I do actually take an interest in some important political issues – if your country is making a really major decision, do you not have a duty to know whether it is the right thing to do or not? But, when it comes to other domestic political views, who wants to hear what I have to say?"

"Bahir, I hope you will get better soon and come back to the meditations," said Peter.

"Well, Peter, when you're 78 years old, I think it's all downhill from here! So don't rely on me. Sometimes, all you need to do is just prepare one or two questions or play some video of the Master. From that video, you can ask people if they have related experiences. Also, it is a mistake to think that the old disciples have all the best stories. The spiritual path is ever new; the Master is always with us in spirit. The experiences and stories that the young disciples have are just as inspiring as our old recollections, if not more so. Also, it's not always the actual details that are as important as the spirit of the speaker. Sometimes, you get up on the microphone, and you speak so fast and enthusiastically, I have difficulty hearing what are saying. My hearing aid can't keep up! But, at the same time, how much joy I am getting from your youthful energy, dynamism and devotion to the Master."

"Bahir, Alex warned me you are very good at flattery, but at the same time, it is encouraging to hear this."

"There is no flattery, it is all true!" said Bahir.

# Getting up early

Daniel was a relatively new disciple and he would often bump into Bahir at the local café, where they would often end up talking.

"Hi Daniel," said Bahir, "How have you found Ashram life in your first year?"

"It's been an amazing year," said Daniel, "I never thought life could change so much for the better."

"That's good to hear," said Bahir.

"But, there is one thing I struggle with," said Daniel.

"Only one thing!" interjected Bahir, "You must be doing very well. I have so many things to struggle with!"

Daniel smiled. "Well the older disciples are very kind, but my Ashram leader tells me the Master wanted us to meditate at 5am. But, somehow, I never seem to manage it, so I feel I'm letting the Master down."

Bahir replied, "Well I remember when I was a new disciple and I read in our Master's writings that 5 am was the best time to meditate. Since I was very enthusiastic, I thought I would set my alarm for 4.45 to try and meditate. So, the next day I get up early – and it's so quiet and peaceful at the time. It was a really new experience, I never knew this time of the day existed! I then understood why the Master recommended that time. So, I sit down to meditate, really hoping I would experience my best meditation. And well, the first five minutes were pretty good; my mind was so peaceful. But after five or ten minutes – what happened? Yes, I started to fall asleep! So much for my best meditation ever!"

"To be honest, I was quite disappointed as the same thing happened the next day too. Fortunately, in the evening, my meditation was much better."

Daniel replied, "Yes, it's a bit like that for me too. I'm not used to being awake at 5am – except for my former student days when we would say up all night partying!"

Bahir said, "For quite a few years I struggled to meditate in the morning and getting up early was a real challenge. But, then I went to see the Master in his main ashram and it was even harder! The Master's functions would often go on well past my usual bedtime, but the idea of leaving the function so you could get up early – didn't cross your mind. You always wanted to catch every minute you could with the Master – even if it meant disrupting your usual routines. I also learnt that some of the Master's most senior disciple were – let us say – not natural morning people either!"

"But, if the Master says we should meditate at 5am, should we not do it?"

"Yes, we can definitely try. Punctuality and regularity in meditation are very important. If the Master asks us to meditate at 5 am, we should aspire to achieve this – and if we can, we should. It is always good to follow the Master. However, at the same time, we have to use our wisdom. Our Master wants us to meditate at 5am – so we will experience greater peace and joy because at that early hour nature is more peaceful. But, if the body is genuinely tired and we get up at 5am to spend an hour nodding off at our shrine – will we experience any of that peace and joy? If our meditation at 5am is useless, but we meditate well at 6am – do you think the Master would prefer we stick to a rigid rule?"

"An interesting question is why did the Master say "I want all my disciples to meditate at 5 am? This is my understanding.

The Master always wanted to offer the highest spirituality in the hope – we would aspire to this. If the Master said 'you might find you have a better meditation at 5am.' Perhaps we wouldn't take the Master so seriously and feel everything is optional. If we think everything is optional – human nature always takes the easiest approach! If we have the capacity, we can be strict with ourselves, but just because we find it easy to meditate at 5 am – doesn't mean it is necessarily appropriate for everyone else. It is one of those things we have to know our capacity. Of course, we have to be sincere, if we stay up to 1 am in the morning watching a film, then say it is impossible to get up before 5 am – we only have ourselves to blame! But, if the body is genuinely tired and you feel you need more sleep, don't try to keep up with others just to meet their expectations."

"It is interesting to hear this perspective. But, I still worry I'm sometimes not doing enough in the spiritual life." said Daniel.

"Well, my perspective is not necessarily the right one." said Bahir. "But, don't forget we meditate for joy. To feel a sense of regret or even guilt for missing spiritual disciplines misses the point. We follow the spiritual life because we are aspiring to gain the real abiding sense of happiness. When we feel that inner happiness and satisfaction, we will get the inspiration to keep practising meditation and, perhaps over time, start to expand our meditation and prayers. Following austerities out of a sense of duty are not the spirit of our path. But, at the same time, we should value spiritual discipline because it is the bedrock of any spiritual life."

Bahir continued: "This conversation is interesting and it reminds me of a time when I was with the Master. The Master was speaking to two friends and he said. 'One of you thinks that he is doing very well, and one of you thinks he is doing badly, but actually it is the other way around. The one who thinks he is doing badly in the spiritual life is actually making very good progress.' The Master didn't elaborate, so you can make of it what you want. But, I found it very interesting. My understanding is this. Sometimes we can be inwardly proud of our spiritual discipline and outer activities. We think we are doing a lot, but actually the motive is coming from our ego. We are not trying to please the Master, but trying to show the world what a great seeker we are. So here, we can think we are doing well, but our Master sees it differently. Other times, we may feel we are doing badly – because we get up late – because we feel we are not as pure as we should be. But, in this case, we are being sincere – we are aware of our limitations, and at the same time, we are aspiring to try and transcend them. In this case, will our Master be displeased? He never expects perfection, only the sincere effort to try and make progress. The problem comes when we think we've achieved everything and can relax and be complacent. In your case, you worry because you don't always meditate at 5 am in the morning. But when the Master feels your heart's devotion and sees your dedicated service – this kind of thing pales into insignificance."

"It also reminds me of a story from the Mahabharata. Could I share it?"

"Of course, I'd love to hear," said Daniel.

"That's very kind. I do tend to get carried away with telling stories - going on and on. But you're a patient listener, Daniel."

"This story goes something like this - Arjuna is walking along with his spiritual Master, Lord Krishna, when he sees a man carrying a cartload of flowers. Arjuna asks the man what the flowers are for. But the man is dismissive saying 'I don't have time for you. I must take these flowers to Bishma. Bishma is the greatest seeker because he prays and meditates with such devotion and intensity. Bishma offers 1,000 flowers to Lord Shiva at once and, though he meditates for only two minutes, his meditation is most powerful.' Arjuna is a little mystified, but then, to add insult to injury, the flower man says: 'Bishma is by far the greatest seeker – by contrast, look at his brother Arjuna – Arjuna shows off, meditating for hours and hours – but one day Arjuna will have to realise Bishma has far greater intensity and devotion in his meditation.' Arjuna turns to his beloved Lord Krishna looking for validation, but Krishna says 'No. The man is right – I brought you here for your own illumination. Arjuna, it is not the length of time you meditate – but the devotion, intensity and concentration of your meditation that is all important.' So Arjuna was illumined by his Master and Bishma's 1,000 flowers."

"That is great story," said Daniel. "Does it mean I can go back to the Ashram and tell everyone Bahir says we can meditate for just two minutes a day!"

"Yes! That is excellent idea. I think they will prefer that to my story about meditating eight hours a day!" said Bahir. "On a more serious note, sometimes it is hard to know how we are doing, but evaluating our standard may not be the most fruitful use of our time. If we have real love and devotion for the Master, that is the most important thing. These other outer things will fall into place over time."

"Another anecdote I would like to share. Many years ago, the Master had a sincere admirer, Tom. From afar, Tom would sincerely speak in favour of the Master and explain his Master's philosophy to those who were sceptical to the Master's Mission. Tom did all this on his own volition because he saw and felt something very special in the Master. The Master was so grateful to this friend of the Ashram and dearly wanted to meet him. The Master offered to travel to his city and meet – but can you imagine? Tom didn't want to meet the Master because he felt he was too impure. The Master was sad and said – 'who really understands what purity is?' So we may think we are impure or useless disciples – but this can be just false modesty and not a true reflection of our real nature."

"It is very inspiring," said Daniel "It is like the Master can see beyond our outer imperfections. It also reminds me of something Alex read out from the Master's writings recently. It was something like – 'This month, let us not think about our mistakes, but only concentrate on the good things we have done.' That was a very useful reading and helps to put many things in perspective."

"Yes," said Bahir. "The Master's philosophy places great emphasis on concentrating on the light, growing into the light. This is how we make progress - because if we get happiness from remembering the good things we do, we will be inspired to try and do more. Rather than be depressed for meditating late, concentrate on the fact you did meditate for half an hour. If you get inspiration from meditation, then over time, it will be easier to get up."

"What about you Bahir? is it easier to get up at 5am now you are the better side of 80?" asked Daniel.

"O yes. Much easier. But I cheat a little by falling asleep in the afternoon! Never had the time when I was a young man! But, I think this kind of thing you're allowed when you're over 80!"

Daniel asked, "Do you have any more stories from the spiritual life Bahir?"

"Many!" said Bahir "But sometimes it's hard to remember a story without some kind of question or comment or ancedote to trigger the memory. These days my mind is like Swiss cheese - full of holes. But, occassionally the stars align and I can recollect events, I had completely forgotten about. Also, a while back, I wrote down a few stories you might like to read. Some of them were written a long time ago, so whether they are worth reading, I don't know. But, I'll dig them out and send them along."

"Thanks Bahir," said Daniel, "and we should do this again

sometime."

"Certainly," said Bahir.

# PART II

# STORIES

# Lack of confidence

After attending a prestigious university, Dennis found himself a good job in the heart of a busy city. But, despite having a promising career and a good circle of friends, he also felt an inner emptiness and lack of purpose. He was 23 years old, but what was he going to do with the rest of his life? This inner turmoil was not something he could easily explain to his friends, who seemed more concerned in getting married, getting a better job and saving up for their first mortgage. But, at this moment, these worldly ambitions seemed unimportant to Dennis.

It was with these thoughts going around in his mind that he stumbled across a free meditation course. Even one year before, he would have dismissed meditation out of hand, but now felt like he had nothing to lose by giving it a go.

To his surprise, he felt a lot of joy from attending this meditation course – even if he felt pretty useless at doing the actual meditation exercises. In fact, he found meditation so difficult, he may have become discouraged, but he also admired the cheerful disposition and self-giving of those who were giving the meditation classes.

At the end of the introductory course, the class givers invited anyone who liked the meditation to continue with an advanced course, for those interested in learning about their spiritual Master and his path of meditation.

Dennis had got used to this weekly meditation and wanted to keep coming, but also felt that perhaps the advanced course was not for him. At the end of the class, the speaker, a chap called Hiran, invited those attending to ask any questions. Dennis was too shy to speak what was on his mind, but a fellow seeker – as if reading Dennis's mind – observed that he did like coming to the meditation, but found it really difficult to control his mind and stop his thoughts.

Hiran gave a sympathetic smile and replied, "I wouldn't worry. Firstly, you have been meditating for just a couple of weeks. You can't expect to overcome a habit of a lifetime in just two weeks!"

Then with a big smile he added, "In my case, I have been meditating for 20 years and I still have difficulty controlling my thoughts!" Hiran laughed – as if failure to control your thoughts in meditation was the most natural thing in the world. "However, although my mind is often unruly. I do feel something inside my heart. In my heart I feel a real sense of joy and peace that has given a different perspective on life."

Dennis felt the obvious sincerity in Hiran. His face really seemed to reflect the truth of what he was trying to say. He also felt there was no effort to impress or evangelise – it was just a spontaneous and heartfelt observation he was sharing.

Hiran continued, "Even if we cannot fully control our mind and thoughts, we should not think we are failing at meditation. Even if the mind is still active, there is another part of us – our heart – that is experiencing real meditation. Of course, if we can silence our mind, our meditation will be infinitely deeper and more meaningful. But, even with a small step in meditation, we can start to feel a transformation. In order to be healthy, we don't have to eat the perfect gourmet food every meal. As long as we eat something, we will grow and become stronger. It is the same with meditation. As long as we eat something, we will be nourished. The problem comes when we don't eat anything at all."

"Our Master teaches it can be hard to judge the standard of your own meditation. It is a mistake to be too hard on yourself. A good sign is: how do you feel afterwards? If you feel happy, if you feel goodwill to the rest of the world, if you feel inspired to do something positive and become a better person, then this is a sure sign that you are doing the right kind of meditation."

"So don't judge your meditation by the number of thoughts that appear. Just concentrate on your heart and try to feel the presence of your inner divinity."

Dennis felt illumined by this answer. It described his situation perfectly and he now placed a much greater value on his general feeling of happiness after the meditation class.

Even the next day, he still felt an afterglow from the previous meditation class, so he decided he would continue to the next course and see what it would bring.

# Choosing a path

Rahul had tried a few different spiritual groups, going from course to course, but the path of this particular Master felt different. Reading the Master's writings, Rahul felt a strong sense of affinity and an unexpected familiarity with the writings – even though he hadn't seen them before. The pictures of the Master in meditation suggested an ineffable sense of poise and peace – the Master's eyes giving a glimpse into a world Beyond.

Rahul had a little understanding of spiritual paths and spiritual Masters, and this Master's teachings on purity, sincerity and simplicity were just as he expected. If anything, the Master's teaching on the value of celibacy helped to convince Rahul he was a genuine spiritual Master.

Although he was comfortable with the teachings of the Master and could see their necessity for a spiritual path, Rahul wasn't sure it was something he might actually want to do himself. With a wry smile, he remembered the thought of St Augustine: "Dear God, please make me pure, but not just yet."

As the course ended, the remaining seekers were asked if they might like to apply and experiment with following the path of their Master.

On the one hand, Rahul was loving the meditations and felt that he really wanted to keep coming. But, on the other hand, it wasn't in his nature to make any kind of commitment – let alone one to try and adopt a spiritual lifestyle.

The disciples of the Master who were giving the classes were very kind, self-giving and there was no sense of pushing their path or way of life. It was offered with confidence, but also detachment. But, this only served to make the path seem more attractive to Rahul.

As the group chatted at the end of the class, Hiran – who was giving the class – spoke to another seeker and said: "As there are many rivers leading to the sea, so there are many different paths that lead to the same goal. Our path is just one of many. If you look around, you may find that another path is maybe more suited to your needs."

Rahul felt in no rush to leave. He was still absorbing the peace and joy of the evening meditation – though at the same time he had uncertainties about what to do. As the other gentleman left, Rahul was left with a just a few members of the ashram who were giving the classes. In this situation, he felt quite comfortable to talk, and with a genuine sense of gratitude for the classes so far said: "I really like coming to your meditations, but I'm not sure I am ready to make a commitment to the requirements of your path."

Hiran smiled and said, "Sometimes it is best to focus on the present moment and not worry about the future. With our path, you can try for as long as you like. If, in a few weeks or months, it no longer gives joy or satisfaction, you can easily go back to your other life and you won't have lost anything – but perhaps you will have gained a useful experience."

Rahul smiled. It certainly seemed less intimidating when it was put like that.

At this point a man, Sachit, from the back of the room spoke. Rahul had hardly noticed him during the past few weeks – he wasn't sure if he had said anything at all. Sachit asked: "May I ask if you feel an inner connection with our Master?"

Rahul replied, "Yes, when looking at his picture, I feel he has attained a high state of meditation and this is a great inspiration to my own meditation."

Sachit broke out into a rare smile and replied, "This is excellent. If you feel an inner connection to our Master and if you have good meditations, then this is a sign that the Path may work for you."

Now Sachit had broken his silence, he continued with an effortless and surprising enthusiasm. "The real spirituality is about experiencing joy from our meditation. If we get this joy from meditation and our spiritual lives, then we will find that everything else falls into place. If you get joy from so called spiritual disciplines, it will no longer be something you do out of duty, but something you look forward to doing. Our Master teaches us to always focus on the light. If we worry about our weakness, insecurities and problems, we only make them stronger, but if we concentrate on light and joy, then we will make progress and our challenges will diminish."

Rahul felt greatly encouraged. Sachit may be quiet, but when he spoke it seemed he had something worthwhile to say. Rahul inwardly felt a strong wish to follow this Master's Path. But, at the same time, he had a reluctance to articulate it verbally. Sidestepping the topic he asked Hiran, "I couldn't help notice that you gave the previous gentleman slightly different advice to myself."

Hiran smiled and said, "Yes, that gentleman is very nice, with a really good heart, but I feel at the moment he is interested in trying different groups and paths. To really make progress in spirituality, we have to choose one path and stick to it. If we go to the Buddhist group one week, then at the same time try a Sufi group, our progress will not be satisfactory. If we want to cross a turbulent sea, it is best to stick to one boat. Jumping from boat to boat mid-crossing helps neither the traveller nor the sailor of the boat."

"And, if you may forgive me for saying, I do feel you have a real sincerity and connection to our Master's Path. Over the years, I have seen hundreds of seekers – if not thousands – and I definitely don't say this to everyone!"

Rahul felt quite exhilarated – not only did he feel that he had found his Master, but here was a community of really good people who seemed to embody the teachings and light of their Master.

# Meditation and dedication

Jenya and Kalap were good friends who both followed the same spiritual path. However, they had quite different temperaments. Jenya liked meditation and spiritual discipline, whilst Kalap was more gregarious and gravitated to working on big projects.

On Kalap's birthday, their Master invited Kalap to his house for a birthday meditation. Also, his dear friend, Jenya was invited as well. Jenya loved to see his Master go into trance and offer his light and love to his disciples. Although it was not his birthday, he felt great oneness with his brother-disciple Kalap's birthday-blessing.

After his Master came down from his lofty trance he offered his love and gratitude to Kalap, but then the Master became more serious and he added: "My dear Kalap, I am very happy with your dedication-life and service to my mission. When I need selfless service, you are there cheerfully and selflessly. But I would also like you to pay more attention to your inner-life – your daily meditation and prayer. Please don't neglect to meditate."

Kalap nodded in agreement and his friend Jenya was secretly quite pleased. Although he would never say anything outwardly, Jenya couldn't help noticing his good friend's meditation was often fleeting to say the least.

Jenya also took his Master's words to heart and he sought to pay even more attention to his own meditation. He made a new effort to meditate several times a day.

Now it happened a few weeks later that it was Jenya's birthday and his Master offered him a very soulful meditation, which helped his aspiration to be elevated to a new height. However, after the meditation, his Master looked more serious and said, "My dear Jenya, I am very happy with your aspiration and meditation, but I want you to be more willing to take part in my manifestation. If I ask my disciples to help spread my light, you cannot do that by just sitting at your shrine. Everything has its time and place. You will meditate in the morning and evening, but manifestation and selfless service are equally important on our path. We need both arms and both legs to run the fastest. Is my philosophy clear?"

Jenya nodded in agreement and this time it was Kalap's turn to be secretly pleased. He would never say anything outwardly, but he did wonder why Jenya would sit and meditate in the Master's meditation hall, when the other boys were outside busy fixing the leaking roof.

The room fell silent as the disciples absorbed the Master's silence. But, after a while, in a lighter tone of voice, the Master added, "You can believe or disbelieve me, but when you work devotedly and selflessly for my outer manifestation, you will get the benefit of my own meditation and sadhana. When I was young, many hours I spent in meditation. Never feel that by working for my manifestation, you are missing out. It is the greatest blessing to take part in God-manifestation opportunities."

The disciples felt grateful for having such a Master.

Then the Master became less serious and began joking with the disciples who were sitting in his room.

As the Master was enjoying innocent stories, a disciple shared a story about another spiritual group featured in a magazine. "Master, it says here this group meditate for at least four hours a day!"

"Four hours a day," the Master said with a big smile. "I guess my path is the path of 30 minutes meditation! My disciples are so lucky they only have to meditate 30 minutes!"

The disciples were not quite sure if the Master was joking or being serious or perhaps a mixture of the two, but they always felt in the seventh Heaven of delight when their Master was in this mood.

# Working in the world

Arjun followed a spiritual path that involved living and working in the world. There was no ashram per se, but the disciples supported themselves by working at various jobs in the local community.

After joining his Master's Path, Arjun was able to find a job at a local private college. It was relatively low paid and the organisation a little chaotic. But, even this worked in Arjun's favour – there was little paperwork and flexibility to take days off. This suited Arjun, and more than compensated for the low income, which was just enough to meet his needs.

Arjun found he enjoyed teaching and, in many respects, he could treat it as an extension of his spiritual life. With his colleagues, he was reticent to talk about his spiritual path and kept his spiritual beliefs very much to himself. Nevertheless, the other people at work somehow picked up that Arjun did a bit of meditation and, since he was vegetarian, assumed he was a Buddhist. Although this was not strictly true, Arjun didn't feel the need to explain why this label was not quite correct.

If time and privacy allowed, Arjun would take the opportunity to have a short meditation during the workday. He felt it enabled him to reconnect with his spiritual practice and the sense of inner peace from his morning meditation.

There were often minor problems and conflicts at this college – leading to frequent complaints by staff and students. However, Arjun felt quite detached from these issues. He diligently tried to do his job, but remained largely unmoved by the daily dramas of working in the college.

By cultivating equanimity and cheerfulness, other members of staff viewed him in a positive light. Quite often they would unburden their complaints on Arjun, who was a patient listener. As much as possible, he tried to look on the bright side of life and encourage people to make the best of the situation. This positive attitude and energy was much appreciated. Though, at the same time, Arjun also felt it was impossible not to be affected by the problems and negative energy himself.

Because Arjun was well-liked by other members of staff, they would often ask him out to social evenings after work. He genuinely liked the other members of staff but at the same time was hesitant to go out with them to a bar.

Since he had become interested in meditation, he had lost interest in drinking alcohol and felt an evening of socialising was something that no longer appealed to him. He didn't want to directly say 'no', so he tended to make excuses that he was busy. Needless to say, he didn't quite tell the whole truth. He thought that saying, "I'm busy sitting still in meditation" would sound a little strange!

Also, it wasn't just alcohol that made him reluctant to attend. On this particular spiritual path, the Master requested his disciples to stay single so that they could fully focus on the spiritual life. His Master felt that a lot of energy and time was required for the romantic life, and this energy and emotional turbulence could easily conflict with the inner peace and equanimity that is the goal of the spiritual life.

In his earlier student years, Arjun found dating had been a draining experience. When Arjun embraced the Master's spiritual life, he felt it was liberating in that he no longer had the mindset of striving to find the 'right' partner. He felt it was much easier to be himself and not worry about what other people may think. However, his particular life choice wasn't something he really wanted to explain to his friends from the office. He just found it easier to focus on his own life with his spiritual community.

However, at the end of the year, the staff made a concerted effort to get Arjun to come to the Christmas party. A long time in advance, they told him the date. He felt a sense of duty to go and felt perhaps it wouldn't be so bad after all.

As he approached the venue, Arjun felt a bit like he was going back in time to his former student days. It was all slightly disconcerting and, after arriving, he felt quite self-conscious sipping a mineral water as his friends enthusiastically downed their first round of drinks.

The noise and atmosphere were quite draining. He felt he was making a lot of effort to fit in, but there was an underlying lack of sincerity in his words. In the environs of this party, Arjun felt torn. Part of him wanted just to leave; another part felt he ought to stay. He was caught by a powerful indecisiveness – he was neither enjoying the moment nor able to leave. He excused himself and went outside for a breath of fresh air. Even leaving the bar felt like a weight off his shoulders. The air was so much freer outside. Not knowing what to do, he took out a small picture of his Master and just looked at it – with thoughts racing around his mind. Arjun wouldn't call it meditation, but it still felt a relief.

He realised that it was a false sense of duty to stay. If he left, who would really notice or remember in the morning? So he just walked away and didn't look back.

The next day he felt he had definitely done the right thing by leaving early; he had put in an appearance, and realised he hadn't been missing out on anything in the past few years. Arjun had moved on a lot from his former student days; he had started to see a glimpse of a very beautiful inner world. Now he had the taste for spiritual food he found he couldn't enjoy his previous worldly experiences in the same way. There was no sense of loss, just a realisation of the profound change in his life.

That day, his meditation was mostly useless, as his mind was inundated with unhelpful thoughts going round his mind – ruminations of the previous evening. But, fortunately, the day after his spiritual community had organised an outing. There was meditation, races, games, food and music. The contrast between the two environments was most striking, and Arjun realised where he felt at home. The joy of spending a day with his spiritual brothers was the best antidote to his inner turbulence created by the previous days experience, and he found this day of fun really helped him get back into his meditation.

# Misunderstanding

Henry and Alan were good friends in the spiritual life, but they had different interests and temperaments. As a result, they often saw things from different perspectives.

On one occasion, their Guru gave a short, informal talk on how the Supreme often put people together who had differing personalities. The Guru explained that when we live and work with people of contrasting personalities, it can force us to face up to our own weaknesses. Even if we find it difficult living and working with certain people, it can help us to transform a part of our nature that we would otherwise ignore.

Their Guru also taught that real spirituality is not just seeking peace in meditation, but trying to slowly and steadily transform our human nature. Also, he warned that rather than trying to avoid difficult people, we should see the potential the situation gives for our own personal growth.

Henry inwardly smiled. He knew intuitively the Guru's philosophy was absolutely true – even if, in the heat of daily life, it was a challenge to actually practise. He also wryly smiled as he thought of the different attitude his housemates had to keeping the house tidy!

\*\*\*

One day, Alan sent Henry a text message about a new idea, which he thought could be a more efficient method to organise the Ashram.

Henry didn't know how to respond to this text message because he didn't think it was a method their Master would have wanted. Their Master was no longer in the body so it wasn't absolutely clear-cut. But, unable to articulate the nuances of the issue and feeling a bit put out, Henry left it and didn't reply – though it stayed in his mind and he ruminated on the issue for several weeks.

After a while, the issue came up again, but it was a little awkward. Due to a lack of communication, each had projected thoughts and ideas about their friend's opinions. It was now more difficult, as they inwardly felt divided over the issue.

Finally, Henry made an effort to speak; and, with a stumbling start, expressed his reservations about why he didn't think it was such a good idea. Alan was sympathetic to his friend's sincerity and point of view; and in oneness with his friend's concern, he was happy to shelve the idea as he could now see the idea from a different perspective.

The conversation was mutually very helpful and helped to fix an inner tension that had been around for the past few weeks.

Henry also felt a little humbled because his mind had rather run away with itself imagining negative scenarios of disagreeing with others in the ashram. It wasn't the first time his mind exaggerated negative potential outcomes, and he was really glad to get out of this negative pattern of thoughts.

It also reminded both Henry and Alan the value of taking time to speak in person and avoid brooding on potentially awkward issues – and why their Guru placed real importance on speaking with your friends.

# Living together

Arjun and Cahit were good friends, but living together presented its own unique challenges. Arjun soon realised that in terms of tidiness and cleanliness they had different perspectives. It was a little ironic for Arjun because his mother used to frequently berate him for being messy when he was growing up. Now, rather belatedly, he understood his mother's perspective and felt a little guilty for his past uncaring attitude. But, with the evangelism of a recent convert, he wasn't happy if things were a mess in his own house. As a result, he often found himself cleaning up after his friend, but at the same, he resented having to do it. In many ways, Cahit was an excellent friend – kind, dynamic and cheerful. Yet Cahit's cheerfulness wasn't always sufficient compensation for Arjun's frustration at living with this situation.

Arjun was also annoyed with himself for how much it affected his consciousness – he felt he should have greater equanimity in dealing with the situation; he didn't always deal with it like he would have liked.

Once he mentioned it in passing to a good friend, Sachin.

"Sachin, I really love visiting your house. It has such a good vibration, you can feel the Master's presence here."

"Well that's very kind, Arjun. How's it working out living with Cahit?"

"Fine. Cahit's a good chap. Only we do seem to have different approaches to cleaning the house."

Sachin laughed – as if reading between the lines.

"So, who does the cleaning in your house?" asked Sachin.

"Well, we share the cleaning 50-50. Cahit makes a mess. And I clean it up."

Sachin laughed heartily, though Arjun was a little surprised by his own strength of feeling. It was like something inside had forced its way out and found expression.

Sachin smiled compassionately and said, "Yes, Cahit's a very good boy. But we all have our personal foibles."

"Firstly, although it may be a bit frustrating to do the lion's share of the cleaning, it is worth bearing in mind that it's infinitely easier to clean up a house than it is to make someone who is miserable cheerful. What I mean is: Cahit definitely has a weakness in this area, but you could be living with someone else who is clean and tidy, but has some much more serious problems. Everybody gets fed up with their living companions at some point, so we have to be careful what we wish for!"

"It is also worth mentioning that, as a general rule, the Master would say: try and make it work with the people who you are living with. If you move around hoping your problems will be solved, they won't. You will just meet them in another form and in other people."

"However, having said that, if someone else's lack of cleanliness is affecting our living space, then we should endeavour to improve the situation. Our Master really demanded and expected the very highest standards of cleanliness. Let me tell you a story. Once the Master told us in advance he would be coming to expect our workplace – five days notice we had. As you can imagine, we worked so hard in making the place immaculate. We thought there was literally nothing more we could do. The Master came and carefully examined every room – the kitchen, bathroom, our offices – with meticulous attention. After his blessingful inspection, he gave us the grade: 'All right.' I don't know if it would have been possible for us boys to get 'good', to say nothing of 'excellent'!"

"In your situation, maybe the best thing to do is to speak to Cahit and work out some minimum standards of cleanliness and tidiness – especially for shared living areas. Also, you have to be very careful – if you carry around this inner resentment, it is very bad for your state of mind and it is not good for Cahit either. It would be better to outwardly talk to Cahit and express these important issues, rather than nurse an inner grievance."

"It reminds me of a story about our Master many years ago. After a deep meditation, the Master asked people to come up and share what annoyed them about their friends. Can you imagine? The Master asking disciples to speak about the failings of their friends!"

"Well as you can well imagine, we were a little surprised and quite reluctant to say anything! But, out of obedience, some boys did go down and they spoke about what irritated them about their friends. I have to say, it was a bit different to the usual afternoon function!"

"Now this is my understanding of the Master's intention, so you can take it with a pinch of salt. If we nurse unspoken grievances – if we inwardly attack our brother and sister disciples – then it is very damaging to our inner life. But, if we clear the air, it can help create a much more harmonious relationship. Of course, everything has its time and place. The Master didn't mean we should always be telling people what they are doing wrong! But if something is deep inside, that is different."

"Another anecdote I remember. Once the Master was watching a boxing match on TV, because he really admired one of the boxers. But, still some disciples were surprised and they asked the Master why he was watching such a violent sport. The Master replied, 'It is true, boxing is violent – and it goes without saying I am against any kind of violence – but in the inner worlds our vital can be just as aggressive as a boxer, if not more so!' The Master finished by saying how he wished his disciples would cultivate more harmony in both their inner and outer worlds."

Sachin continued: "Going back to the Master encouraging disciples to speak about their frustrations, I have to say it was quite a rare occurrence, and if one had such an intention, you could misinterpret it. If you read the Master's writings, he explains so vividly the importance of being kind and offering goodwill to other people. But sometimes the real kindness is to speak directly to people and make them aware of why they are causing a disharmony."

"Well, Arjun you're very kind for listening to my mammoth talk, I don't know if it makes any sense."

"Yes, very much so," said Arjun.

"Well, if you don't mind, one other story I should share with you, Arjun. When I came to the path, I was worse than useless in the world of cleaning. I thought so long as I was meditating and busy serving the Master, I could leave my room like a beer garden. But once the Master scolded me in a very significant and illumining way. The Master told me directly, 'Sachin, can you not please clean your room? Every night, in my subtle body, I try to visit and bless your soul whilst you are sleeping. But, even in my subtle body, so painful it is to visit when your room is so messy. I appreciate your dedication, and inner aspiration, but we have to give due importance to the physical. If we don't keep our body, house and room clean, we block the descent of the divine forces. Your Master will forgive you, but your own soul will not. Your soul is so embarrassed that my inner beings have to suffer so much because of your untidiness. All that sincere aspiration you are cultivating is diminished because you have left your room in such an undivine state. My dear Sachin, always you have to be ready to welcome your Master.'"

"Well as you can imagine, I felt both suitably embarrassed and also moved by the Master's love and concern. When the Master says he meditates early in the morning for our own benefit, we have to believe this is not just an idle promise."

# Singing with enthusiasm

A few thousand years ago, there was a spiritual Master who lived in India, with quite a few devoted disciples. This Master had also composed a few devotional songs, and he taught his disciples that if they sang his songs devotedly and soulfully it could equal their highest meditation.

At the Master's weekend meditations, he also encouraged his disciples to perform his music as part of the evening meditation.

One evening, a new group of disciples came to visit their Master for the first time. They had been following his path for just over a year, but living many miles away they had not had the opportunity to come before.

During the evening function, some of the Master's older disciples who happened to be accomplished musicians, performed his music. They had been practising their arrangement for quite a few weeks and had raised the standard to a high musical level. During their performance – as he often did – the Master went into trance, and even as the performance ended, the Master barely seemed to come down from his Heavenly state. After a few moments of precious silence, he offered a faint smile, with eyes still half-closed. This was quite common, as the Master rarely commented on performances, preferring to just meditate.

Next to perform were the new group of disciples, who sang the Master's song with no instruments, just singing. Although not always quite together, they sang with great enthusiasm, dynamism, simplicity and joy.

After a fairly short performance, they finished to a generous applause. The Master came out of his trance and was beaming with outer happiness, giving a wonderfully infectious smile. The Master offered rare words of praise, remarking how happy he was to hear his songs sung so soulfully and with such great enthusiasm.

"This is such a marvellous performance! It gives me so much joy when my disciples sing with such enthusiasm, soulfulness and eagerness. I feel this is definitely one of the best performances of the summer!"

Needless to say the new disciples were over the moon to hear such warm words of encouragement – especially since they had been told the Master so rarely gave outer praise!

# Correcting others

Hari was a good disciple. He led a disciplined life and tried very sincerely to follow his Master's guidelines. However, he also felt it was his duty to tell his fellow brother and sister disciples if they came up short and did things in the wrong way. When Hari travelled to an ashram in another city, he created a bit of a stir because he told quite a few disciples what they were doing wrong, and it didn't go down particularly well!

Hari was also prone to periods of mild depression and frustration. He lived the strict spiritual life but felt he wasn't always getting the joy he should be getting.

After ruminating on these issues for a few weeks, he requested a private interview with his Master where he hoped he would be able to air his grievances about what was happening in his ashram. He was fairly confident the Master would take his point of view.

When Hari went to meet his Master. The Master offered him a blessingful smile, which really melted his heart. After a period of soulful silence, the Master began, "My dear Hari, what I would like from you is for you to be happy. You must feel that in your happiness is your spiritual progress. If you are unhappy and depressed, it is like a dead weight that you are placing on top of yourself and you will make no progress."

"Of course, if you are depressed, I will still inwardly offer my compassion and love. But, for my love and compassion to be effective, there needs to be some receptivity. This receptivity is in your happiness. So from now on, please make happiness your highest priority. If you are happy, then you will feel a great weight has been lifted."

It wasn't what Hari had expected at all. He thought the Master would talk about the issues in his ashram. He was moved by his Master's words but also a little taken aback.

As if the Master was reading his mind, the Master continued, "I deeply appreciate your efforts to follow my teachings and guidelines in the spiritual life, but it is a mistake if you feel you are responsible for correcting all the decisions of my disciples. If you spend your time trying to tell others what they are doing wrong, you will only add frustration to your life."

"It is true, I set the highest spiritual standards in the hope my disciples will feel the inner necessity to aspire and follow my approach to the spiritual life. But, even I cannot always be telling them what they are doing wrong. If I corrected a disciple every time they were doing something wrong, I would have left the body many years ago!" The Master and Hari smiled.

After a short pause Hari also asked the Master, "But Master, I thought that if there were problems in the ashram, then we should let you know, before the problem gets worse."

"Yes, those to whom I have given responsibility for my ashram must ensure certain minimum standards of behaviour, and if it is a question of serious problems in the spiritual life – problems with emotional-life, vital-life – then you must let me know so that I can deal with it in my own way. But, we have to use our wisdom and discriminate between serious issues which threaten the spiritual life and those other areas where I have given disciples the opportunity to learn from their mistakes."

"In my ashram, I have disciples of many different standards in the spiritual life. I cannot expect every disciple to have the same kind of surrender. In the beginning, we cannot expect everything of a young child – we need to allow him a certain freedom to learn and appreciate the rules of life. It is the same in the spiritual life – seekers need to feel the inner necessity of making certain changes and approaches to the spiritual life.

But, at the same time, if a young child puts his hand in the fire, then will his parents not immediately tell the child to stop for his own protection?"

Hari was already feeling better – it felt like his Master was taking a load of unnecessary responsibility from his shoulders, plus at the same time, he felt lifted up by the mere presence and light of his Master.

But, his Master had not finished. He continued, "My dear Hari, I'm sure you are aware of the Saviour Christ and his profound message: 'First remove the beam out of your own eye, and then you can see clearly to remove the speck out of your brother's eye.'"

"If we wish to change our brother disciple's behaviour, we first have to lead by example. If we are frustrated and unhappy, pointing out their failings will in no way inspire them to lead a better, more illumined life. First, we have to aspire for light and happiness in all aspects of our being – our mind, heart and soul. Only then will we begin to have the potential to improve standards in the ashram. But, if we want to change someone's nature, rarely can that happen by barking at people!

However, if we can bring down abundant light and peace into our nature, then at least some people will either consciously or unconsciously start to be inspired by our example. So this is what I want you to do – please be happy. Happiness, happiness, happiness! Leave the correction of your fellow man to God. Your only job is your happiness and spiritual progress!"

# Reincarnation

Many years ago there was a spiritual Master who had quite a few disciples. As a general rule, this Master did not believe in showing occult power, as he felt the only forces that could help transform human nature were divine love, divine concern and divine compassion. However, sometimes the Master would use his intuitive capacities to tell interesting stories and, on occasion, give his disciples hints about their previous incarnations.

However, after a few years, the Master felt this practice was not helping his disciples, but could cause problems of jealousy and pride. On one occasion, the spiritual Master asked for spiritual questions, but to the Master's disappointment, quite a few disciples were just wanting to ask about their past or future incarnation. The Master responded to one of these questions by saying: "The spiritual life is all about the present moment. It doesn't matter what we achieved last week, last year – to say nothing of what you might have done in your last incarnation. The important thing is to aspire to be more sincere and soulful in your present spiritual life. Knowing about past incarnations mainly feeds our curiosity. So from now on let us not worry about the past or future, but concentrate on the golden opportunity we have in this present moment.

\*\*\*

Arjun came to the spiritual path a few years later, and he heard these stories second-hand from other disciples. Yet, he was also intrigued by the subject and inwardly held a desire to know about his past incarnation.

A few months later, Arjun was at a meditation function with his Master.

It was a most soulful atmosphere; time seemed to pass

effortlessly as if the thin veil between Heaven and earth had momentarily lifted. Arjun felt transformed to another state of consciousness where the usual attractions and anxieties of the world lost their lustre, leaving him feeling perfectly calm and inwardly still. It was a rare feeling to be so at peace with the world.

At this point, the Master spontaneously asked for any spiritual questions. Arjun vaguely remembered his old desire to ask about his previous incarnation, but in this state of mind it seemed unimportant – even churlish. Arjun just continued to sit in a meditative frame of mind and was amazed at the Master's capacity to answer questions in his own inimitable way.

Alas, by the next day, the sublime beauty of his previous meditation had faded from Arjun's mind and his old thought patterns had risen back to the forefront of his awareness. In his mind, he felt he had missed a golden opportunity and he inwardly said to himself he would definitely ask next time.

A week later, Arjun was again at the meditation with just a handful of other disciples, and despite feeling a good sense of peace, he was ready to ask. However, the Master never subjected himself to any particular routine, and this time did not invite any spiritual questions. Arjun thought: fine, the Master is bound to ask next week. However, the next week, again the Master ended the meditation without inviting any questions. It seemed the Master had lost interest in inviting questions from his disciples.

Arjun told himself, "I should really stop bothering with such a silly thing like knowing my past incarnation." But, at the same time, the thought still lingered. So the next week, he started to pray for illumination – thinking perhaps the Master would give him a sign in a dream. After a while, he stopped praying and was just concentrating on his meditation. Then to his wide surprise he had an image in his mind of an old farmer tending a field of rice. Although he didn't really recognise the person, he had the strong feeling that this was one of his past incarnations.

Then the image faded and it was replaced by the image of an old farmer digging up potatoes against a backdrop of a bleak, windswept landscape. Then this image faded to be replaced by that of a fisherman riding over the waves of the sea. Then he saw a soldier in a uniform marching off to war. With this, he got the point – his past incarnations were neither interesting nor illumining. The desire to ask his Master about his past incarnations faded, never to return.

\*\*\*

However, the story didn't quite end there. A good ten years later, Arjun was travelling with his Master in Myanmar on a spiritual retreat. Arjun was moved by the serenity and calm of the country; with this different pace of life and the inherent spirituality of the people, meditation felt much more natural and effortless. He was also fascinated by the Buddhist monks who, every morning, went begging for food.

Rather unexpectedly, the Master initiated a conversation and suggested to Arjun he should go and invite the head monk of a local monastery to come to one of the Master's functions. Arjun followed the Master's wishes. He really enjoyed visiting the monks and speaking about his Master's Path and its similarity with Buddhism. The monks gladly came to visit his Master, and Arjun received much joy from this soulful oneness between different spiritual paths.

The next day, with a faint smile, the Master said to Arjun, "Perhaps in a previous incarnation you meditated with those monks." The Master's smile widened and then he walked away.

Arjun was very happy, though at the same time he felt grateful to be on his Master's Path – with its great variety and scope for transcendence in so many different aspects of life. He felt in a monastery he would not be able to make anything like the progress he was making on his Master's Path – even if, at the same time, escaping to a Himalayan Cave did have a certain appeal!

# Inspired by sleeping disciples

Thomas had been following the spiritual life for many years. As part of his spiritual life he used to get tremendous joy from running. He was never particularly good at running, but the exercise and challenge was a great way to break up the day and get out of his mental thought processes. However, outer circumstances left him in poor physical health. Becoming less active was quite challenging as it left a gap in his life that was hard to fill. He made conscientious efforts to get better, but to no avail. Thomas tried sticking with one doctor, but after a few months of no improvement, he tried a different doctor. Every health practitioner saw it from a different perspective, but nothing seemed to work. His Master taught that it was good to pray for better health, but at the same time, we have to be surrendered to the result. It was a little frustrating, but the only thing he felt he could do was to accept and make the best of the situation.

With more time on his hands, he took to trying a bit more meditation during the day. After a few weeks' perseverance, he felt a real sense of newness and joy in his meditation, and it started to fill the gap left by the end of his outer running. Encouraged by the glimpse of inner joy, he made greater efforts to focus on his meditation. For quite a few months he strived to deepen his concentration and awareness – though, on his own, progress could feel slow.

A few times a year, he travelled with his fellow seekers to a foreign country for a spiritual retreat. It was a mixture of meditation, food, music, plus other spiritual activities.

On one particular holiday, his rhythm of daily practice and japa went out of the window, and he didn't have the chance to practise his usual meditation exercises.

Yet, despite making relatively feeble efforts and being concerned with some outer problems, in the meditation room he started to feel a surge of joy coming from the heart.

No matter what was happening outwardly – formal meditation, plays or music of differing standards – the joy was the same.

Towards the end of one late evening function, he couldn't help but notice how quite a few of his fellow brother disciples were falling asleep for the final meditation. Usually, this behaviour would be discouraging and distracting, but on this occasion, the joy of the heart made any outer events all but insignificant, like passing birds leaving no mark on the sky.

It was no personal effort or achievement, but it felt like the grace of his Master was accentuated by the presence of his brother and sister disciples.

For Thomas, it was a valuable lesson – it is easy to be frustrated with outer imperfections, but when you meditate well, all these problems fade into insignificance. It gave him his first glimpse that the spiritual delight is entirely independent of what other people are doing or thinking. It was also a reminder of the importance of the sangha (spiritual community). Never had such grace or meditation been present in his lone meditation at home. Even the sleeping disciples seemed to bring forth, with greater intensity, the very tangible presence of his Master.

# Following the crowd

There was a spiritual Master who lived in a busy city, where he held meditations for his disciples. However, every now and then, he liked to escape the hustle and bustle of the city to enjoy the peace of Mother Nature.

On one occasion, a group of visiting disciples were taking the subway system to get out of town. They were in a cheerful mood as they were looking forward to a day with their Master in the country. At the first interchange, a disciple got off the train and everyone else followed.

As the next train entered the platform, Arun got on the train to ask the conductor where the train was going. However, it turned out the person wasn't actually a conductor – just someone dressed very smartly. However, in the meantime, all the other disciples followed Arun and got on the train. With fifty disciples on the train, Arun assumed it must be the right one.

Everyone was so busy chatting with their friends they did not concern themselves with train timetables or direction but assumed someone else would know where it was going. However, after a few stops, Arun realised: "Oh no! We are going in the wrong direction!"

The great joy and excitement of the disciples was burst as they realised they would have to get off and go back where they came from. Unfortunately, it took over an hour to catch up with this mistake and they arrived at the picnic spot, just as the outdoor meditation was finishing.

As the meditation and prasad was finishing, the Master invited disciples to share good news or stories.

Arun felt miserable, as he felt partly responsible for arriving late, so he reluctantly got up to tell the story of woe. Much to Arun's relief, the Master found the story very amusing and his Master's laughter was infectious in lifting the spirits of those disciples who were frustrated for missing the meditation; they now felt just as joyful as after a good meditation.

But, after the Master's infectious laughter died down, he also became inspired to speak more seriously. "My dear children, this story is amusing, but also illumining. Your cheerfulness and oneness I deeply appreciate. Recently, so hard you worked for my concert and your spirit of oneness was most significant. The concert was both an outer and inner success and I offer my deepest gratitude for your service."

"However, when you go back to your respective countries, you have to be careful to make sure you do not get on a train going in the wrong direction. Just because you see an experienced disciple behaving in a certain way, doesn't mean necessarily, he is doing the right thing. Before embarking on a new project, the most important thing is to begin with the right spirit and make sure you are striving to please me in my own way. If you follow blindly what others are doing, you may not always be going in the right direction."

The Master went silent and a visiting disciple asked, "Since we live so far away, it is sometimes difficult to ask you directly what is the right thing to do. If we cannot ask you directly, how can we know what is the right thing to do?"

The Master smiled and then replied, "Firstly, you should try to keep your mind calm and quiet, and then meditate. Try to meditate without any preconceived notions or expectations. You may not get an answer straight away, but if you sincerely try to please God in His own Way, definitely He will guide you inwardly and outwardly. Secondly, please read my writings. In my books you will see answers to many questions that have been asked over the years, and even if you don't see a particular question, my consciousness is definitely in my books and writings. If you can absorb part of my consciousness through reading my books, definitely it will help you know what to do."

The Master paused and the disciples sat rapt in attention and silence; then the Master continued, "Also, just now I warned about blindly following other disciples, but don't go to the other extreme and make the mistake of trying to be self-sufficient with a haughty independence. Before starting a project, you should your share ideas with good disciples. Ask in a spirit of openness and humility, and if others have reservations, you can re-evaluate your decision. It is better to take the time to create an enthusiastic oneness than to rush ahead with your own plans and ambitions."

"If you can make decisions collectively and with a spirit of humility, definitely you will be more likely to do the right thing and please the Supreme in me."

The Master's seriousness melted away, and he reverted to the joyful attitude of a few minutes before. With a big smile, he asked: "So Arun, which train do we need to take to get back into the city?"

"Yes Master, I shall meditate very deeply before getting the train home this evening!"

"Very good, Arun!" said the Master.

# New disciples

Many thousands of years ago, there was a fully realised spiritual Master. After attaining God-realisation, he would have been content to spend the remainder of his years meditating in a Himalayan cave. However, he felt an inner Command from the Supreme to offer a spiritual path for those seekers who also aspired for God-realisation.

The spiritual Master had infinite love and compassion for his disciples, but at the same time he was conscious of his inner promise to the Supreme to guide his disciples to their ultimate liberation from the meshes of ignorance. As a result, the Master was a combination of inner sweetness and outer strictness. For those who joined his ashram, he expected a sincere commitment to the spiritual life. In particular, he taught his disciples to distinguish between the fleeting and unreal pleasures of desire and the real satisfaction that comes from the inner aspiration.

After a few years, the Master gave a short talk, where he expressed his wish for the ashram to expand and find more souls who had an affinity with his spiritual path. However, after this talk, the Master felt an inner resistance from some of the established disciples, so he felt the need to give a further talk. "Some of my disciples worry that if we gain more disciples our spiritual standards will slip. Or perhaps they worry if we have more disciples they will receive less attention, and my love and concern will be diluted."

"But, this is not he case. I feel there are souls who are really hungry to join our spiritual path. If new seekers join our Ashram, it will bring in new energy, new aspiration and brush away a feeling of contentment and complacency some of my disciples have unfortunately developed. Also, my divine love is very different to the ordinary human love. It is true that human love is limited. If we love one person, it feels there is less for another person. But, divine love is not like that. Divine love is unlimited and can only expand by touching more people. So from now on, please feel the necessity of bringing more seekers to our path. If you are sincere in your effort to bring in new seekers, you will also see the benefit in your own spiritual life."

"Inspired by the Master's words, some disciples began giving talks and meditations in nearby towns. The experience was richly rewarding and, as their Master predicted, they felt the benefit to their own spiritual life. However, when they began to share the requirements and expectations of the Master's Path, many good seekers dropped away."

The disciples were somewhat discouraged by this and they reported their experience to the Master. The Master smiled compassionately. "Firstly, I am very grateful for your dedication and selfless service, but please don't be discouraged – even if your classes are outwardly unsuccessful. I'm sure you are aware of our great spiritual classic *The Bhagavad Gita*. In our Gita, Sri Krishna utters the immortal words, 'We have the right to action, but not the fruit thereof.' When giving lectures, we should give them very much in this spirit and place the results at the feet of God."

"Also, even if seekers do not join our path, it is maybe the case that we have sown the first seeds in their spiritual journey. You have no idea how introducing my philosophy and meditation can change people's inner lives – even if they don't become my disciples."

The Master paused and he appeared to go into an inner silence. No one dared move, rapt in attention. The disciples were deeply inspired by the divine philosophy of their Master and their previous frustration now seemed entirely misplaced.

After a pause, the Master began speaking again. "Now I would like to say there is one more thing we can try. When we tell seekers about our path, we can't necessarily expect them to follow our path straight away. Seekers may take time to feel the inner necessity of following our lifestyle. If we expect too much, too soon, they may feel our path is inaccessible and not give it a try. However, before they join the main ashram, we can give them some time to follow our path to the best of their ability – as long as they understand what is ultimately expected from our path."

"In this period, it is really important that we do everything we can to inspire and encourage the new disciples. By making friends with new seekers, they will gain the confidence that they too can follow our spiritual life."

"Also, when giving classes, it is a mistake to harbour a feeling of superiority or the feeling you are more advanced in spirituality. This spiritual pride is a real mistake. If seekers feel there is a wide gulf between your standard and their standard, they will be discouraged. We have to give lectures with real humility – if new seekers make mistakes, we should not criticise, but say and feel that when we were new, we also made this kind of mistake. It is this humility and oneness which will make seekers feel they are part of our spiritual family."

Again the disciples were amazed at the Master's insight and profound understanding of human nature. With renewed enthusiasm, the disciples went out to give new lectures and encouraged those interested in following their Master's Path to try without any expectations.

After a few years, a few new disciples had wholeheartedly accepted the Master's Path, and – just as the Master predicted – brought new inspiration, enthusiasm and joy to the Ashram. Some of the older disciples sincerely felt a renewed interest and aspiration in their own spiritual life from the energy of new seekers. At the same time, the new disciples were inspired by the stories and experiences the older disciples shared.

However, since they had given so many lectures over the years, some disciples still felt very discouraged that the Master's mission was not growing as quickly as they had hoped.

On one occasion, the Master invited informal questions. Arjun spoke up and said, "Despite all the concern and patience we have have offered to new seekers, at the end of the day, the requirements of the Path are often too much, and since our numbers are almost stagnant, perhaps we should relax the standards to make it easier for new seekers to join the Ashram."

The Master remained silent and with a serious expression replied, "Arjun, I appreciate your sincerity, but at the same time it is a serious mistake to feel that if we relax our standards, it will make it easier for people to become my disciple."

"You can believe me or disbelieve me, but if you offer a relaxed version of my path, if you try to dilute my spirituality, the souls of potential disciples will curse you. The souls of my disciples are drawn to my path, to accept me in my own way. We should never be embarrassed by our code of life and our approach to spirituality. It is by coming up to my standard that the soul will feel the inner divinity of my Path. If we offer a diluted form of spirituality, they may not feel anything special and we will be doing a real disservice to new seekers."

"Also, we have to be careful. Sometimes when disciples want to relax the standards of the path or present my spirituality in a modified form, it is because of their own insecurities and uncertainties. Sometimes we project our own weaknesses onto new disciples and assume they will not want to do what we have difficulty doing ourselves."

"If you give meditation classes, you are pleasing me – it is true. But if we give classes we have to maintain a very high standard in our own spiritual life. We cannot ask others to do what we can't do wholeheartedly ourselves."

"My dearest Arjun, so hard you have worked over the years to bring seekers to our path. How much I appreciate your sympathetic oneness with new seekers. Many of my disciples talk and have good intentions, but you simply do. So this I deeply appreciate. However, it is important to remember you are on a very special spiritual path. Have more faith in your Master and more faith in your spiritual Path, and let us leave the results at the feet of our Lord Beloved Supreme."

Arjun sat as if pinned to the back of his chair, digesting the words and spiritual force of his Master. Inwardly he marvelled at the spiritual depth and foresight of his Master, and for a moment it brought him right back to the feeling he had when he saw and accepted his Master for the very first time, many years ago. It reminded him why he accepted his Master, and he intuitively knew that his Master's words and teachings were coming from the Supreme himself.

# God's Love

Swami Adeshananda was a spiritual Master from India who lived many years ago. After attaining God-realisation, he founded an Ashram on the outskirts of a busy city. Many seekers came to visit this Guru as they felt something special in his demeanour and meditation. However, although many admired from a distance, he did not attract too many disciples. On the outer plane, he was always scolding and barking - not just his disciples - but even those who came to see him. He was strictness incarnate and was not afraid to speak his mind. Once a big-shot local politician came to offer his pranam to the Master, but Swami Adeshananda treated him like an ordinary person and did not even look at him. The local big-shot politician never returned!

Yet, although he was always scolding his disciples, he had tremendous affection and love for the animal kingdom. Swami Adeshananda would befriend any stray animal and offer them the greatest love, affection and concern. The Ashram was a veritable sanctuary for all kinds of birds and animals.

Once his disciples were sitting at the feet of their Master when they had the opportunity to ask him a question.

"Master, it sometimes appears you have more love and affection for animals than you do for humans," asked a disciple.

Swami Adeshananda replied: "What do you mean sometimes? Is it not the case that animals are infinitely better than humans? Humans think they are the most evolved species, but often the only thing that has evolved is their sense of pride, their sense of jealousy, their sense of superiority. Now these stray animals that I look after in my Ashram are by far my best disciples - they know the meaning of obedience and they don't answer back! True, the animal kingdom fights, but not on the scale of humans. Only the human species is capable of mutual self-destruction."

In response, another disciple asked: "Master it seems you are always displeased with us. Why do you not just give up on us?"

Swami Adeshananda paused and appeared to go into meditation. His eyes rolled up - as if he was going to a place beyond the world of time and thought. Across the Swami's face was a countenance of sublime peace - completely unruffled by the cares of the world. For quite a few minutes the Master remained absorbed in this inner silence. His disciples went quiet, trying to join in their Master's sublime meditation. Then, the Master's eyes flickered as if he was returning to the earthly plane and he began to speak, but his disciples were wonder struck - the usual barking tone of the Master was replaced with a soft and ethereal voice that seemed to be coming from a different plane. The Master's face glowed as he spoke to the disciples.

"It is true I bark and scold, but do you think that is my real inner nature? Outwardly I bark, but inwardly I see you as another living God. It is because I love you unconditionally, that I seek to transform your stubborn human nature. When I bark and shout, you have to know this is but a mask to cover the real and powerful love that I have for all of God's Creation."

"If I was to give up on you, then the only failure would be myself. I see you as part and parcel of myself - your weaknesses are my weaknesses; your achievements are my achievements. It is not a question of choice. I have accepted you as my very own and have made a solemn promise to the Supreme to lead my disciples back to God. Until you have all attained liberation, I will work either on earth or from Heaven to free you from the meshes of ignorance. For better or worse, your existence and my existence are inseparably one. For better or worse, your existence and my existence are inseparably one. You could choose to delay your journey. You could physically leave me.

Even then, in spirit, I will be with you - whether you go up to the highest Heaven or down to the lowest hell. Of course, I want you to go up not down. But, if you fall down to the lower vital worlds, I will have to go down one level further so I can lift you back up."

The Master paused and the disciples did not want to break the silence. It was rare for the Master to speak so openly and candidly.

The Master continued.

"The reason I bark and shout is that I only want sincere seekers who are willing to take responsibility for their spiritual life. I'm not interested in attracting large numbers or appealing to the ego of humans. Recently, a big shot came to our Ashram, but I could feel inwardly he expected special attention and praise. But, in God's eyes, what does his worldly status mean? Some people think they are doing so much for the world and they are such great people, but when they go to the other side - I tell you, they will get the shock of their lives! But, the lowest person in earthly prestige who works with humility and devotion will be taken to the very highest Heaven. Did not the Christ say 'But many who are first will be last, and many who are last will be first?'"

"In my philosophy, God takes many forms and has infinite divine qualities. But, if I had to define God in one word it would be love. How dearly I would like my disciples to feel God's love for them. If you could love yourself in a divine way - even for one minute, your life would be changed forever. Divine love is the greatest force for it transcends the ignorance of the world and only spreads and expands. From now on, don't pay attention to my barking and scolding, forget your own mistakes and weaknesses, but only focus on God's love; for that alone will undoubtedly save you."

"My dear children, you know I don't often speak like this, so please take these words to heart. You can forget my scoldings sooner than the soonest, but never forget that God's love is very real and tangible. You say you can't feel God's love because he hid it from you. But, where did he hide it? Did God hide it at the bottom of the ocean or the top of Mount Everest? No. He hid it in your own heart. So let us stay in the heart, always in the heart.

# About the Author

Tejvan Pettinger was born in Runnymeade, UK in 1976. From 1995-99 he studied PPE at Lady Margaret Hall, Oxford University.

In 1999, he became a disciple of the spiritual Master Sri Chinmoy. He is a member of the Oxford Sri Chinmoy Centre where he offers meditation classes.

Tejvan Pettinger's previous books include:

*Happiness Will Follow You* (2010) Ganapati Press.
*Walking Along the Sunlit Path - Tejvan's Stories* (2011) The Goldenshore.
*Cracking Economics* (2017) Octopus Press.
*What Would Keynes do?* (2018) Octopus Press.

Tejvan is an amateur cyclist and competes for Sri Chinmoy Cycling Team. His results include:

- UK National Hill Climb Championship - 1st (2013)
- UK National 12 hour Time Trial Championship - 2nd (2016) 284 miles.
- UK National 100 mile TT Championship - 3rd (2014)

www.ingramcontent.com/pod-product-compliance
Lightning Source LLC
Chambersburg PA
CBHW021109080526
44587CB00010B/454